CINEMATIC GAME SECRETS FOR CREATIVE DIRECTORS AND PRODUCERS

CINEMATIC GAME SECRETS FOR CREATIVE DIRECTORS AND PRODUCERS

Inspired Techniques from Industry Legends

RICH NEWMAN

ELSEVIER

AMSTERDAM • BOSTON • HEIDELBERG • LONDON • NEW YORK • OXFORD
PARIS • SAN DIEGO • SAN FRANCISCO • SINGAPORE • SYDNEY • TOKYO
Focal Press is an imprint of Elsevier

Focal Press is an imprint of Elsevier
30 Corporate Drive, Suite 400, Burlington, MA 01803, USA
Linacre House, Jordan Hill, Oxford OX2 8DP, UK

 Recognizing the importance of preserving what has been written, Elsevier prints its books on
acid-free paper whenever possible.

Library of Congress Cataloging-in-Publication Data
Newman, Rich.
Cinematic game secrets for creative directors and producers: inspired techniques
 from industry legends / Rich Newman.
    p. cm.
Includes bibliographical references and index.
ISBN 978-0-240-81071-3 (pbk. : alk. paper)
1. Video games—Design. 2. Cinematography—Special effects. I. Title.
GV1469.3.N485 2008
794.8'1536—dc22   2008028464

British Library Cataloguing-in-Publication Data
A catalogue record for this book is available from the British Library.

ISBN: 978-0-240-81071-3

For information on all Focal Press publications
visit our website at www.books.elsevier.com

08 09 10 11 12   5 4 3 2 1

Printed in China

Working together to grow
libraries in developing countries

www.elsevier.com | www.bookaid.org | www.sabre.org

ELSEVIER   BOOK AID
            International   Sabre Foundation

CONTENTS

INTRODUCTION

What is Cinematic?

The last ten years have ushered in a whole new era of game development. In addition to the constant influx of new technology and content, the convergence of the film and game industries has pushed game developers to achieve a whole new level of standards in epic gaming. This trend has been illustrated by the increasing number of games that are being optioned into feature films—and more and more films are being translated into video games. Also, with animated features, it is now a common occurrence to see a simultaneous release of a film and game (*Bee Movie* and *Beowulf* are just two recent examples).

In retrospect, the mashup of these two mediums seems to be a natural one. The gaming industry and the film industry already have many things in common, including similar roles and positions while working in production, comparable production cycles, and many mirrored production concerns. Also, more and more filmmakers are actively becoming involved with the game industry. As this book is being produced, it has been announced that director/producer Jerry Bruckheimer is partnering with MTV to create a game production lab, Steven Spielberg is getting involved with game development, and director John Woo was recently involved with the production of the game *Stranglehold* for Midway Games. The bottom line is that there are many talents that good filmmakers possess that are becoming highly desirable in the game industry today—such as experience with production and a familiarity with story and cinematic techniques.

Making a game more "cinematic" is a hot topic in today's gaming world. For example, writers are now becoming "gaming writers" as the need for more developed scripts becomes more prevalent in production. Also, many film directors and producers are now getting involved with game development because of the need to raise production value in certain titles. Even major game luminaries known for "old-school" methods of game development are turning their attention to cinematic production techniques. The game industry has also responded to this trend by including many of the aforementioned cinematic topics in the major gaming conventions and organizations. For example, the International Game Developer's Association has now added a top-notch special interest group concerning the subject of game writing, and the 2007 Austin Game Developers Conference had an entire track dedicated to writing for games. The same can be said for current trends regarding game cinematography and direction.

In the past, "cinematic" simply meant an in-game animation that usually told part of the story to the gamer (also known as "cut-scenes"); these scenes usually consisted of one to five minutes of noninteractive viewing meant to draw the player into the world of the game, but usually did just the opposite, as the gamer would be on the sidelines watching the action. Now, "cinematic" is a general term used to describe many of the techniques used in the film industry for video game production. The immediate perks of using these techniques are obvious: Why pull the player from the game to watch a cut-scene when you can incorporate good filmmaking techniques throughout the game play and keep the player immersed in the game to experience a deeper emotional impact?

Typically, when a producer is working with a cinematic mind-set, there are several specific things that he/she has in mind: higher-production-value moments within the game vs. cut-scenes, better story and characters, and professional cinematography. Each of these represents a major challenge for the game producer, but can make significant improvements within a game title. Other examples of cinematic production that we will discuss in this book involve the use of epic music and sound design, the use of celebrity talent (and directing them), and creating better levels through the use of framing, blocking, and camera movement.

As this book is being written, there are twenty to thirty video games that have been optioned and are currently being developed for films by various production companies all across the United States. Because the game industry is now very aware of the possibility for crossing over into film, many new games are being conceived and developed from the very beginning with a cinematic mind-set. The marketing potential of these game titles is obviously doubled when you consider the possibility of a title hitting the big screen in addition to the home console.

This book is for game producers, creative directors, and students who wish to pursue a career in creating cinematic games; whether you are fresh out of school, or you simply wish to inject your current thinking with some new ideas, I hope the techniques used within this book will assist you. Most of the methods and ideas listed in these pages are tried and true, having been used throughout the film industry for decades. The application of these techniques will help you create a deeper gaming experience and a higher production value in your game.

For students/younger producers, I have also included a quick primer on the current production models in game development and a section on creating an independent game and company. Though a game can be an expensive endeavor, the availability of free/inexpensive software and raw talent has made indie game development much more accessible.

Part 1

GAME INDUSTRY PRIMER

1

THE PRODUCTION PROCESS

Upon initial contact with the game industry, you may feel a bit overwhelmed by the sheer amount of responsibility involved with creating a new game title. In addition to the pressure associated with creating a game that will sell well and be received with enthusiasm by the gaming public, the actual work involved with development weighs in heavily. These responsibilities include working with the game's budget, streamlining the production process, and managing a team and assets that grow and change on a daily basis.

A typical game title can cost many millions of dollars and involve a very long-term commitment (sometimes as long as four to five years), so the pressure to create a franchise or successful title can be massive indeed. Understanding the production process allows you as a game producer to roll with the inevitable changes and challenges that come with the development of a game and empowers you to manage your project efficiently. More importantly, it will allow the game to be completed, which is always a plus when dealing with game publishers!

Utilizing the cinematic skills of a filmmaker in addition to the usual game development model within the various phases of game development allows you shape the project into a more marketable and, hopefully, more enjoyable title. But first, let's take a look at the typical development cycle.

1.1   Lifecycle of a Video Game

Like most creative processes (such as making a movie, creating a graphic novel, and so on), the game industry has a definite process and lifecycle involved with a new project. In the video game industry, the process of creating a new title pretty much follows this cycle:

- Concept/R&D
- Preproduction

- Production
- Testing/QA
- Postproduction

Each of these phases will be discussed in greater detail in later chapters, but here is a quick rundown of what's involved with these various stages of game development:

The *concept phase* of game development is time spent defining the game that you are about to create—both creatively and technically. This time involves choosing the type of game you are going to make—RPG (role-playing game), FPS (first-person shooter), MMORPG (massively multiplayer online role-playing game), and so on; determining the game elements and features that will be involved in game play (story, characters, game options, and so on); and working out the details for the future marketing of the title, such as the genre of the game (horror, adventure, and so on), the platforms/consoles the game will be played on, and the game's projected rating. This collaborative process usually involves the producers, lead designers, and the creative director of the game.

The concept phase usually ends with the creation of a tangible risk analysis report, a mission statement that will unite the production team in creating the design, and possibly a prototype version of the game (sometimes called a "vertical slice"). In most cases, these elements are compiled into an overall production plan that will be pitched to the perspective publisher to get a green light for the project. A typical pitch includes the materials listed earlier, along with a design document, a project plan, and a budget (sometimes called a "cost forecast"). Once the budget and schedule have been approved by the publisher, the game then moves on into pre-production.

The *preproduction phase* most closely mirrors that of the film industry; it is at this stage that the story is developed and honed, the look of the project is fleshed out using art and previsualization techniques (like storyboarding), and the budget and schedule are defined for the coming production cycle. Although this is called "preproduction" in the film industry as well, in the game industry, preproduction also includes defining all the technical requirements of the game (such as design, art, and features), prioritizing features and specifying constraints (usually influenced by the budget and schedule), and creating a basic design document. These steps constitute the very roadmap that the production team will follow during the many months of development.

If you have not yet developed a prototype of the game, this is also done during preproduction. Though the finished prototype will be a playable level of the game, which can begin as simply as mapping out the game idea on paper. Once the prototype is honed to a coherent representation of the game concept, it is developed into an actual demo.

Another key element of preproduction is hiring the team that will be involved with production. Beware: the hiring process can be a long one—and it's not uncommon for larger production studios to tackle the lengthy task of hiring prior to the creation of the game's concept! At the very least, allow for a reasonable amount of time to be used in getting the right members of your team. Once the design document is in place with the prototype, and all the personnel have been hired, the game can then move into production.

The actual *production phase* of development is usually composed of coding, generating, and implementing assets into the game; also, any unfinished details regarding the game's design will be finished as well. It is during this phase that any required motion capture/voiceover work, music, and basically anything else that is involved with making the actual game comes together. This is the longest phase of game development and usually tests the strength of the overall production plan. Keeping the production team on point and out of meeting overload can be the biggest challenge for a producer as the need to keep up with current gaming trends becomes increasingly important. Sometimes the woes in a schedule revolve around the discovery and implementation of new features in the game—this is called 'feature creep' and can cause studios to spend an excessive amount of time and money during production.

It is important to track and monitor the progress of the game throughout the game's production; publishers demand up-to-date reporting on schedule and budget concerns, as well as on any issues developing with the game's production. Usually, a project management program (such as Microsoft Project) is used to assist producers with tracking the game's progress, though you may have to tweak the program in order to fit your needs (you will want to spend the bulk of your time actually managing your project rather than working with the software). There will usually be an online version of the game's production cycle as well that the team can access to see what is happening in the other departments of development (for instance, the art department may want to see the status of coding the assets into the current build of the game). Setting small milestones or goals for each production task is a great way to determine whether a particular item has been completed and is the industry standard measure for tracking completion.

The next step in the production cycle, the *testing/QA phase*, is very different than that of the film industry. Where a film may undergo a series of audience tests, screenings, and so on to get feedback (sometimes referred to as "research"), a game is thoroughly evaluated throughout the production phase by a quality assurance (QA) team for bugs within the title. Every time a new asset is introduced to the game, the QA team gets a crack at it. Any time a new tool or game element is introduced, QA quantifies its value. At the end of development, a title must get approval from the QA team during the code release process before it is sent on to the publisher (in a form sometimes referred to as a Gold Master) for approval.

Though testing/QC is often thought of as a process that occurs at the end of production, the truth of the matter is that the testing of a game occurs throughout the development cycle. As a matter of planning, it should be determined early in the production process whether an internal or external QA team will be utilized during the development of the game, as this decision can affect the schedule and budget immensely. This phase usually ends with the QA department comparing the final product against the original game plan to determine its validity (Alpha and Beta testing), and the release of the final version of the game (sometimes called "code release" or the Gold Master). At this point, your moves on to various locales for approval.

In addition to getting the game to the publisher, the manufacturers of all consoles the game will be played on must approve the title as well. All major platforms will have their own sets of criteria that must be met for the game to be approved for release on their console. Also, the game must be sent to the Entertainment Software Rating Board (ESRB) to receive the game's rating. Without a rating, most major software vendors and retailers will not carry your title. If the game is being released in other countries, it will also have to be sent to the appropriate ratings boards in those locales. Once the game has been give the thumbs-up by all concerned and you have received the official rating of the game, the final version of the game can now be sent to the publisher. The next and final phase of development is known as postproduction.

The *postproduction phase* in the world of game development is slightly different than that of the film industry. Although this phase is generally typified by filmmakers as the editing and cutting of a movie, in the game industry this phase signals to the team that the game is pretty much finished. Postproduction in game development means creating "closing kits", which archive the title (sometimes games get rereleased at a later date, so it's important to keep the game and all its elements intact), discussing the aspects of the production process that went right/wrong in lengthy postmortems, and documenting the creative process that was involved with creating the title so that future games can be developed more smoothly within the studio.

Depending on the features of the title, the complexity of the programming, and the size of the team and budget, the production cycle for a video game can be anywhere from a few months to several years. Usually the length of production is based upon the choices you have made in the game design. One of the earliest decisions you will make when producing a game is the type of game that the team will be developing.

1.2 Types of Games

The evolution of games is a fascinating subject. With origins that are deeply rooted in arcade-style games, the game industry has evolved over the last few decades into a realm of many different game styles and genres. Though most of the game types we commonly see today originated in the 1980s, there are still new game styles emerging on a regular basis. The types of players/gamers have also evolved during this period.

Gamers today have a way of micro-organizing game genres— as the field becomes more diversified, more and more types of games are appearing on shelves. It is important to know these various types of games, if for no other reason than to realize there are many different types of gamers; a player who loves first-person shooters will not be as attracted to a football game as a sports gamer. Although this is not a complete list, here are the several major types of games that are being developed:

- First-person shooter (FPS)
- Role-playing game (RPG)
- Massively multiplayer online game (MMOG)
- Massively multiplayer online role-playing game (MMORPG)
- Third-person shooter
- Real-time strategy (RTS)
- Sports
- Action (racing, fighting, and so on)
- Simulation
- Casual/arcade

The FPS is hands down one of the two most popular genres. With origins deeply rooted in the early games of id Software (Doom, Quake, and so on), the shooter has come a long way. Developers like Ubisoft and Bungie have made titles like *Tom Clancy's Ghost Recon*, *Halo*, and *Tom Clancy's Rainbow Six* household names. The entire concept of the FPS is that you are always looking down the barrel of your weapon from a first-person perspective. Usually, this means a military/gunman-themed game or a hunting title.

It is arguable that games that utilize the first-person perspective typically get more of an emotional payoff when the game is completed, so developers love to create these types of games. But don't let this dissuade you from choosing one of the other formats; every player has his or her own preferences and there have been successfully produced titles in every style and genre.

Blacksite: Area 51 by Midway Games is an example of a first-person shooter. Reproduced by permission of Midway Games. All rights reserved.

The RPG is also a popular game type, though it is slowly being usurped by the MMORPG. With its history firmly rooted in the world of the PC gamer and old-school pen-and-paper games (like *Dungeons and Dragons*), the RPG appeals to players who want to interact with more of the world around them in many detailed ways. This style of game is also popular because of the many ways that a gamer can approach a level, customize characters, and create their own in-game stories (usually because of a more open, "sandbox" style of game play). Typically, this game is tailored to the fantasy/sci-fi crowd, but newer titles are slowly changing this. The 2006 award-winning game *Elder Scrolls IV: Oblivion* proved that the RPG is still alive and kicking—and this title also has spawned a new wave in first-person perspective RPGs versus the usual third-person view.

The second most popular genre in gaming, and possibly the hottest trend in the game dev world at the moment, belongs to the MMORPG. Using all the strengths of the RPG, these games

Elder Scrolls IV: Oblivion: an award-winning RPG from Bethesda and 2K. The Elder Scrolls IV: Oblivion® © 2006 Bethesda Softworks LLC, a ZeniMax Media company. All rights reserved.

have taken role playing to the next level by moving them online. Titles like the popular *Lord of the Rings Online* games take players and hurl them into a virtual world where thousands of players interact within the same sandbox. Obstacles that held the MMORPG back in the past, like a limited, PC-based audience and small multiplayer modes, have all but evaporated with the widespread availability of broadband Internet and the capabilities of consoles to now include online gaming. The ability to create add-ons and modules later on to a game is an additional strength of the MMORPG (though it is not limited to this genre—modules were created for games in the 1990s as well, including *Quake*, which was an FPS). A great way for young game designers to get experience in the game industry is to create "mods" for games like these.

Lord of the Rings Online Shadows of Angmar, Book 12: The Ashen Wastes by Turbine, Inc. The artwork appearing above is copyright protected and reproduced with permission. © 2008 Turbine, Inc. All rights reserved. This publication is in no way endorsed or sponsored by Turbine, Inc. or its licensors.

When the popular *Tom Clancy's Ghost Recon* game series switched from a first-person perspective to a third-person perspective, fans of the popular franchise collectively groaned, but after they played the new games, they embraced the style and fell in love with it. This game quickly became one of the first successful third-person shooters. Ubisoft's latest installment, *Tom Clancy's Ghost Recon: Advanced Warfighter 2*, was one of the hottest titles of 2007 and has proven that looking over one's shoulder does not necessarily mean taking yourself out of the game. In fact, the perspective allows the gamer to see some of the more complex moves the character has at his/her disposal, and even maximizes the use of certain obstacles. Deciding on the game perspective that you will use in your title will be one of the biggest decisions you will make when constructing your initial game concept, as this will affect the camera angles and framing that you can use within your game levels.

Tom Clancy's Ghost Recon: Advanced Warfighter 2 by Ubisoft. Reproduced by permission of UbiSoft. All rights reserved.

When a gamer thinks of RTS games, no title comes faster to mind than the popular *Command & Conquer* games. Appealing to the crowd that wants to control every aspect of their world, these games offer a god-like role to the gamer and are sometimes so complex that a player may spend months getting the nuances of the game straight. An RTS game is about unfolding the game play in real time—meaning that you must construct bases, finish levels, and so on—while the game is moving with you at the same time. The RTS has taken a hit in popularity over the last few years, but again, with the use of broadband Internet and sandbox play, the RTS is destined for a comeback. Many developers are taking the concept and play of the RTS online and taking the genre to the next level.

Command & Conquer 3: Tiberium Wars. © 2008 Electronic Arts Inc. Electronic Arts, EA, the EA logo, Command & Conquer and Command & Conquer 3: Kanes Wrath are trademarks or registered trademarks of Electronic Arts Inc. in the U.S. and/or other countries. All Rights Reserved. All other trademarks are the property of their respective owners.

Though there's no need to explain what a sports, sighting, or racing/flying game is, it is important to note that these are still relevant and strong genres. The Madden football titles still consistently perform for Electronic Arts, and even some of the older, more established fighting titles like *Mortal Kombat* by Midway Games are still cranking out new versions and selling them. It's the straightforward approach of these games that make them popular to gamers—and it's also the trait that makes them appealing to developers. They are also some of the highest-grossing titles of all time, with broad marketing appeal and phenomenal sales numbers.

Ace Combat 6: Fires of Liberation. ACE COMBAT® 6: FIRES OF LIBERATION ™ © 2007 NAMCO BANDAI Games Inc. All trademarks and copyrights associated with the manufacturers, aircraft, models, trade names, brands, and visual images depicted in this game are the property of their respective owners, and used with such permissions. Courtesy of NAMCO BANDAI Games America Inc.

The final major category of games we will discuss is another PC-heavy genre: the simulation game. Game guru Will Wright made his name in the game industry with the popular *Sims* games of the 1980s and 1990s (though the game is more like an RPG than a simulation-based game) and even now has the industry buzzing with glimpses of his new title, *Spore*. A typical simulation game is quite different than Will Wright's creation, though.

Microsoft has dominated this genre with the always-popular and always-available flight simulation programs/games. In fact, entire magazines have been devoted to fans of these flight simulators. In the future, look for more titles to follow in the footsteps of *The Sims* and for more of them to migrate from the PC to consoles (*The Sims* game has actually already been developed for consoles). "Virtual reality" games like *Second Life* have also contributed to taking the Will Wright–style sim genre to a new level.

Will Wright's new game, *Spore*. © 2006 Electronic Arts Inc. Electronic Arts, EA, the EA logo and Spore are trademarks or registered trademarks of Electronic Arts Inc. in the U.S. and/or other countries. All Rights Reserved. All other trademarks are the property of their respective owners. EA™ is an Electronic Arts™ brand.

With each game genre presenting its own set of challenges and strengths, choosing the type of game that you will be creating is one of the most basic yet important steps you will undertake early on the development process. Staying true to the basic concept of the type, yet innovating new approaches to the genre, will be the razor's edge the production team will tread upon. Decisions regarding the title will be made using a steady stream of innovations, assets, and a diet heavy with brainstorming.

1.3   Brainstorming and Initial Decisions

Once you have decided upon the type of game you will be developing and you have made some of the major decisions regarding perspective and platforms/consoles, it's time to get that creative team together and to start brainstorming. This is a habit that you should continue throughout the development process. Entire meetings will be dedicated to hashing out the finer details of characters, locations, and game elements/features. Starting this habit in the concept phase of development kicks off one of the best practices that you can use throughout the lifecycle of the game (and this is part of most major development models such as Agile Development). It should be noted, though, that meetings cost money! Assembling a group of your major salaried employees together for hours on end can really start running up the tab on your production, so keep the meetings important, concise, and timely.

Managing a brainstorming session means keeping focused, staying on the agenda, documenting the finer points of the meeting, and involving everyone concerned. Learning the finer points of conducting useful and concise meetings is something beyond the scope of this book—and many great books have been written on the subject. It is well worth your time to delve further into this subject.

Though the development team will have other tools at their disposal for collaborating with the producers (Web sites, email, scrum sessions), nothing beats a good brainstorming session for getting a project back on track quickly. Keeping the meetings relevant helps prevent the team from getting demoralized by attending these sessions, too. A typical unproductive meeting usually means that nothing of use was actually generated or the participants felt like their input was not needed.

Everyone attending a brainstorming session should be encouraged to contribute to the development of new ideas—and though criticism is usually discouraged at these sessions, it is important that all the team members give honest feedback to ideas that are presented there. Because attendees will often represent whole slices of the production team (engineers, artists, sound/music, and so on), it is a necessary practice to incorporate all these areas into these sessions. These brainstorming meetings ensure that as the game progresses, current ideas/trends will be incorporated into the title and the game will stay current and fresh. They will also bring a sense of a shared vision throughout the production team and ensure that the title will be created with a unified concept.

It should also be noted, though, that although it is important to receive and consider the input of everyone on your team, it is more often the original vision of the creative director/game creator that must be disseminated throughout the production team to keep the game on track. Much like a director/producer of a film, the decisions of the creative key provide the compass that the production will follow.

1.4   Using Game Theory

Game theory is actually an older concept that was developed in the 1940s to study the decisions that players make when presented with a choice. The book *Theory of Games and Economic Behavior* by John von Neumann and Oskar Morgenstern (Princeton University Press, 1944) introduced the idea that when players are playing a game, they will always choose the path that offers the most gain to the player. Besides being used to develop games, this theory has been applied to economics, animal behavior, and sociological issues.

When planning your project, game theory can be a great tool to use when placing the gamer in situations where choices must be made regarding the fate of the game's protagonist (again, this is a great subject worth reading more about—pick up Neumann and Morgenstern's book for a lot more detail). These choices all have consequences (good or bad, whichever is determined by the designer) and spawn new directions in which the game can travel. Also, as a game producer, it is important to keep this theory in mind when reviewing the game's design documentation, the story, and game play features.

Another major factor to consider when using game theory is the idea that players begin all games ignorant of the rules of that game. A game's concept must include the information regarding how a gamer is to learn these rules and guidelines, and how strategy, difficulty, and opposition will be used. Decisions regarding these important areas should be made with the intention of maximizing the enjoyment of the gamer—a concept that is known in the game industry as "play-balance". A great way of approaching this is to think of ways to create your game without the use of an instruction manual. The use of game theory can also create great suspense and surprise within the game by defying the typical response of the gamer and tricking the gamer into treading less-traveled paths.

Games that have great critical moments, memorable antagonists and opponents, and decisions that bring great returns make for spectacular games. It is also the idea that the player has chosen his/her own path and personally achieved the particular outcome of the game that makes video games so popular. It is this very concept that makes gaming interactive. Game theory is

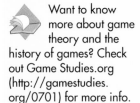

Production Tip

Want to know more about game theory and the history of games? Check out Game Studies.org (http://gamestudies. org/0701) for more info.

a basic concept that every game must incorporate to some degree and must be addressed while defining the concept of the game.

Interview: Game Design and Theory: Noah Falstein, Game Developer Magazine

Noah Falstein

Noah Falstein heads The Inspiracy (http://www.theinspiracy. com), a consulting firm specializing in game design and production. Since 1980, he has designed and managed entertainment and educational software titles for companies such as Williams Electronics, LucasArts, The 3DO Company, and Dreamworks Interactive. He has written the monthly design column for *Game Developer* magazine since 2002 and serves on the advisory boards of the Game Developer's Choice Awards, the Serious Game Conference and the Games for Health Conference. Some games he has designed or codesigned include *Sinistar*, *PHM Pegasus*, *Indiana Jones and the Fate of Atlantis*, and design contributions to the recent the *Star Wars* RTS, *Empire at War*.

Newman: On your Web site The Inspiracy (http://www.theinspiracy.com), you are in the process of creating a list of 400 rules concerning game design. At the minimum, what core guidelines/advice would you give a game designer concerning the creation of a new, successful title?

Falstein: That's tough to answer briefly—creating good games is a hard job, and there's a lot of knowledge and skill involved in doing it well. But to take "at a minimum" to heart, here's the core advice I would give: learn from what has been done before in your chosen genre, but be sure to innovate as well. Keep your game elements as simple as possible. Decide on a creative vision for the project, get buy-in from the rest of the team, and stick relentlessly to the purity of that vision (or if you change it, make sure that change is reflected in everything that has been previously done on the game). Get the core game play up and running as early as possible, and test it repeatedly with both the team members and regular "new blood" fresh testers. Don't release it until it's great! That's a lot to ask, but it's a good formula for success.

Newman: Do you think that games with well-defined goals/missions make a greater entertainment impact upon a player than games with lots of open/sandbox-type play?

Falstein: No, both types can be valid; it depends on the audience you are aiming at as well as a lot of variables about the game genre, your team, your schedule, and other things. It's a little like asking "Will dishes with meat taste better than vegetarian ones?" or even "Does salt taste better than pepper?"—the ingredients aren't as important as the way they are combined and whom the final dishes are prepared for. Well-defined goals are generally a good idea for most games, and particularly so for the more casual players. Open-ended games often demand more imagination and initiative from the player, and are best when the world is familiar (like *The Sims* or *Grand Theft Auto*). One good compromise is to give a game a fixed goal, but provide multiple ways to reach or achieve it. Some very successful series of games like *Diablo* and *Civilization* have used formulas like that (even though the two are quite different in game genre and play mechanics).

Newman: A lot has been said about the psychology of game development—particularly in the area of choices that are presented to players, and the decisions they make when presented with a choice. This is the core of game theory. What are other ways that game designers can tap into human psychology?

Falstein: Another potentially long list! Just a few examples: the psychology of emotion (for example, for a horror game, how to scare people most effectively), the psychology of perception (how to make individual icons or buildings or tools instantly recognizable to a player), evolutionary psychology (what type of story elements are we humans hard-wired to care the most about?) and more. Psychology is very closely intertwined with good game design. Many game designers I know are quite familiar with psychology and often well-versed in related areas like neurophysiology, learning theory, and evolutionary psychology. Understanding how the brain works is very helpful when you're trying to craft an experience for a player.

Newman: When you're playing a new video game, and you find yourself losing immersion/suspension of reality, what's usually to blame? How can we prevent this from happening?

Falstein: Good game design always has to contend with the twin demons of Boredom and Frustration at the edge of the Flow Channel (see the book *Flow* by Mihály Csíkszentmihályi (Harper & Row, 1990), a great reference for designers). Boredom occurs when the challenge of the game does not increase in difficulty and variety fast enough to keep the player engaged, and frustration occurs when it gets *too* difficult too fast. Frustration can also result from inconsistent interface, bad dialog and story, confusing directions—all sorts of things. One of my pet peeves for example is games set in the distant past, or far future, where everyone talks like a person from the present day.

Newman: When you get involved with a new project, what ingredients do you look for in the concept package that signals to you that this will be a great game?

Falstein: Unfortunately, that's a luxury I can't often afford—as a freelancer, I am often brought into an existing project because it is having trouble, or at least needs something to improve it, and the companies that know how to turn out great hit titles (Blizzard, for instance) don't often turn to outside design help because they have quite enough expertise in-house. But it's often not the concept that suggests it will be a great game, but the team. When I meet a group that knows what they're doing, and that is already following the principles I mentioned previously in my first answer, I can be confident it will be at least good and possibly great. When it's a great fresh concept in the hands of someone who knows what they are doing (as when Will Wright first showed his early work on *Spore*) then you know there's the potential for greatness.

Newman: It seems that a lot of games limit their audience by only targeting a specific niche or type of gamer. What types of measures can be taken when crafting your design document to balance having a specific genre with not limiting the scope and appeal of the game?

Falstein: You can't please everyone all the time. It's wise to target a specific type of gamer. The trick is often to use interactivity to widen the appeal—in other words, the fact that in our medium, unlike other traditional entertainment forms like books, movies, and classic TV, we can change the experience based on the specific person (or people) playing. There are many ways to do this—one example is how Blizzard took the "traditional" MMORPG assumption that you need to combine with a group of other players in order to progress your character past the first level or two and turned it around, making it possible for players to do well alone or in a team—and that's certainly part of the success of *World of Warcraft*. But note that despite its success, it hasn't done as well in numbers of players as *Tetris* or *Pokemon* or *The Sims* or the *Halo* franchises—and I expect that there's not a huge amount of overlap among those groups either. The lesson is that you can aim at a specific group of players and still have a big hit—but if you try to make a game that will appeal to everyone in the world, you'll probably fail.

Newman: Do certain game development models (the Iterative Approach, Agile Development, and so on) lend themselves to a better-developed product than others? What's been your experience?

Falstein: Iterative development is behind many very good titles, but it has the dangerous problem of being hard to predict how long it will take. Still, if you are planning on breaking new ground, it is often the best way to go. If, on the other hand, you are simply planning on doing a sequel to a hit title (like the latest *Madden*

Football) then you're probably better off identifying a handful of ways that you intend to improve the game, plan and test them in advance, and build to a strict schedule. The problem of "Who is paying for this and what are their expectations?" is one that no designer can ignore, and it's very rare to find someone who can tolerate (or afford) a lot of flexibility in a schedule and budget.

Newman: What are some of the warning signs early on in development that can signal a poorly designed game?

Falstein: There are many. Confusion about the core vision of the game. A mix of contradictory, ill-fitting game elements. Too much complication and detail. A focus on knowing every detail of the story of the game and dozens of pages of backstory about the characters—but little or nothing about what the player actually *does* in the game. Lots of mentions about "then the player does X" and nothing about what happens when the player chooses *not* to do X—or worse, the player is killed off any time they try something else. Those last two are actually very common when a filmmaker comes to the game experience. Too much enthusiasm for a previous title—"This will be just like *Halo*, only much better"—often with a budget that is 10 percent of the game it is emulating. Too little regard for, or knowledge of previous titles: "This revolutionary game will be the first one ever designed by a woman, for women!" (I've heard that at least five times in my career, and it wasn't true even the first time I heard it). Too much unwarranted arrogance: "I know everything about storytelling, and games all do it badly, so I'll create the first great game with a deep and compelling story—even though it's the first game I've ever worked on."

Newman: It seems that "cinematic" game design is more about finding the depth of immersion in a game visually and sonically that exists in a movie rather than actually making a game that plays out like a film. What is it about creating a video game that now draws the film community (like Jerry Bruckheimer has recently)? What types of lessons learned are brought to the table by film producers?

Falstein: I've worked with a lot of filmmakers over the course of my career. In general, the more they know about film and the more successful they are as filmmakers, the more they realize that games and film are fundamentally different, and although there are things each medium can learn from the other, it's important not to assume that what works in one medium will work in another. I've heard that sentiment, or the equivalent, expressed in conversations I've had with Steven Spielberg, George Lucas, and James Cameron.

On the other hand, I've also seen the opposite side, with people coming from film with an attitude that they know all there is to know about entertainment and they'll "fix" video games and make them "truly mass market"—and these people generally have failed miserably. Spielberg in particular is an avid game player and has been for many years. I have a lot of respect for his abilities, and am hoping that his current collaboration with Electronic Arts will result in some great games. But even when they don't know much about games to start with, the writers, set designers, directors, and producers who approach games with a willingness to learn have been great to work with. They bring a lot of very useful techniques and perspective. Much of film grammar has some application to cinematic games. For example, the emotional significance of camera angles, like looking down at a scene from a height in order to make the characters depicted feel insignificant, can work in games as well as film. And producers in particular have introduced a lot of useful management techniques for handling a huge team of creative and technical artists. As a freelance designer, I am very unusual in the games industry, where most designers are full-time employees, but freelancers are much more common in the film industry, and that is having an effect as game budgets and teams keep growing.

Newman: Any advice for producers/designers out there?
Falstein: One thing to keep in mind when making games that are based on a film or use cinematic techniques, is that games are, at their very core, all about interactivity. It's about what the player does, the choices the player makes, and not about conveying a story or experience to a passive audience. Some of the techniques that work well in cinema don't translate well to games, just as screenwriting differs from writing novels or plays. My view of the core difference between the two has a lot to do with the evolutionary origins of the reasons that people enjoy entertainment.

Passive forms of entertainment like film or novels where the audience sits back and enjoys someone else's story are, at their heart, interesting to us, because we can learn from the experiences of someone else—usually the protagonist of the film. Because the action happens to someone else, we have the luxury of empathizing, and empathic reactions like tears of sympathy for a dying heroine are, if not easy to evoke, at least achievable. Games are more about learning directly from our own choices, and active reactions like the joy of triumph or anger at being thwarted are common. There are few games that make someone cry at a failed romance—but many of them can cause the player to raise their fist and shout in exultation when they defeat a boss monster. Games are often at their best when the subject matter is basic survival, and the choices are well represented by the kinds of images and choices a computer can create and model. So as with any art form, unless you really know what you are doing, it's best to stick to what the medium does best. Once you have become proficient at game design, then you can take more liberties with the game and push the boundaries.

2

UNDERSTANDING PREPRODUCTION

The typical preproduction period for developing a game is very similar to that of the film industry. It means defining the product! For most studios, going into preproduction means that a great, new game concept is on the table and now it must be pitched and sold to a game publisher. This usually means creating a formidable game design document and either a prototype of the game or a vertical slice of what the game will be like—this is usually a single level of game play that will later be used within the finished title.

Key decisions that determine the quality and cost of the game must be made in preproduction—these choices include the number of personnel that will be hired, the length of the production schedule, the features of the game, and honing the final versions of the game's technical and creative design documentation.

The first step is determining a crystal-clear concept for the game. Although different studios/publishers have different formats for this (see the Sample Game Concept in Appendix A: Extras), there are a few required elements: genre, platform(s), basic elements, basic story, and main characters. Usually, a general blurb or mission statement is also included to sum up the overall intention of the game, a risk/competitive analysis is constructed, and a prototype is made.

Basically, the concept includes all the information you need when pitching a game to a publisher. Sometimes, this is best approached by thinking of it as a presentation. Think high-concept and creatively, roll it up into a great pitch, and you have a great representation of what kind of game you are proposing. Once you have finished the basic concept of the game, you can then get into the details of the actual game, or the requirements.

Many games, like *Elder Scrolls IV: Oblivion,* are developed on multiple platforms. The Elder Scrolls IV: Oblivion® © 2006 Bethesda Softworks LLC, a ZeniMax Media company. All rights reserved.

Development Tip

Once you have all the elements of the pitch together, consider assembling it as a Microsoft PowerPoint presentation. Once you are granted a meeting with a publisher, it's always easier to "show" an idea than it is to "tell" it. There are also many great templates for creative presentations on the Microsoft Office Web site. (http: //office.microsoft. com/en-us/powerpoint/ default.aspx)

The concept phase of development is usually marked by numerous meetings to discuss the various features that will be included within the game. These include the artistic elements, the levels and designs that will be used, and the particular game props (weapons, maps, and so on) that will influence the programming and engineering of the game.

A typical way to approach these meetings is to form a list of priorities: high-priority items are the things that set the game apart from others of the genre and that definitely need to be included, and low-priority items are things that basically just gild the lily—in other words, they are items that would be nice in the game, but are not necessarily needed. No matter what priority an item is given, though, all ideas presented should be noted and considered.

It is also during this period that a rough schedule is outlined based on the needs of the game. Because most project management systems rely on time and labor constraints, the team will plan the amount of development that will be involved with implementing each of the items listed in the requirements. Before moving on to honing the final game plan, it must be determined whether the title can be brought in on schedule based on implementing the listed requirements. If it is determined that it can, the team can now focus on developing the final game plan.

The game plan represents the final overall map for developing the title. In addition to the elements already included in the concept and feature list, a game plan also includes a specific budget, schedule, and staffing plan (examples are included in Appendix A: Extras). This is the bible by which your game will be created! Once you have pitched your project to a publisher and they have accepted your game plan, it will become abundantly clear how important staying on schedule and budget will be. Great skills at overall project management always make the difference between successful studios and unreliable studios.

In the film world, there are several elements of preproduction that are similar to those of the game industry. The hard lessons learned by a hundred years of filmmaking (such as working on script development prior to production) can be applied to not only streamline the preproduction process (especially when forming the concept), but to help create a more cinematic product. These will be discussed in Part 2.

2.1   Script Development

There is currently no recognized general format for creating a script in the game industry. Though there are many writers in the field of game writing, there are dozens of different methods by which these writers create a script for a game. Some resemble basic narrative writing (such as a short story), some approach the script much like a graphic novel (this usually means describing short scenes or panels, then listing the dialogue that will occur there), and some have even gone to great lengths to design their own methods for writing the script that can involve detailed hyperlinks and bookmarks that outline the various paths the gamer can take.

In many cases, game developers have relied upon cut-scenes to relay any kind of story to the gamer. These are usually short animated clips that convey a necessary piece of information or relationship within the game to the viewer. Though in some cases these are quite necessary (especially if the story is rather complex), it is the issue of taking players, even momentarily, out of the game play that has caused the game industry to take a second look at cut-scenes. Another factor that must be considered when producing in-game cut-scenes is the need for specific producers and personnel who are skilled in this area. This can contribute to inflating the budget—especially if you are using celebrity talent or directors!

At any rate, whether you use cut-scenes or not, some type of script will be developed to let the production team know exactly what kind of story they are creating. This is important when defining the locations, characters, and style that will be represented within the game. Typically, once a first draft has been developed and read through by the development team, revisions will be asked for. The notes that you take during the initial read-through will be valuable in helping you to craft revisions according to the wants/needs of the team producing the game. The process of writing the script, reviewing the script, and crafting rewrites may repeat itself many times before the final script is approved.

Do not confuse a game writer, though, with the person who creates the game instruction manual! This should be a completely different person (usually a technical writer), and he/she will not become involved with the project until close to postproduction.

Development Tip

Download a demo version of Final Draft or Movie Magic Screenwriter to get a firsthand look at the construction of a script. You can also get a free copy of Celtx—a valuable screenwriting program and script development tool—at their Web site, http://www.celtx.com.

2.2   Hiring the Crew

Depending on the location of the studio, hiring the personnel needed to complete production of a game can either be the easiest of steps or the most frustrating. If you are located in one of the game development meccas (such as Austin, Los Angeles, Vancouver, New York, or San Francisco), crewing up can be as simple as posting the job openings on your Web site and letting the resumes roll in. If you are not in one of the major cities for game development, getting interested (and competent) parties may be a bit more involved.

Typically, a human resources (HR) department takes care of all the hiring for a studio, but if your studio is small (or new), you may not have an HR department in place. That said, there are several different strategies for finding the skilled talent you need: getting a recruiter, posting jobs on popular game job sites, going to the major conferences, and contacting schools.

Hiring a recruiter may be the easiest solution, as they basically do the other three things listed for finding talent. A good recruiter does other things as well, such as screening the applicants, fielding the first round of interviews, and organizing the lists of potential candidates for each position to be reviewed by the production team. Once the recruiter has gathered a number of portfolios, resumes, and work samples, the top candidates can then be scheduled for a more formalized interview process.

If you decide to do without a recruiter, you can post the positions on some of the major game development Web sites and begin contacting schools. Most schools that offer degrees in the various fields of game development have a counselor or administrator in charge of helping find positions for students. Keeping in mind that most people you hire from a school will be completely inexperienced, you can definitely get some great people from the bigger schools for a reasonable price. As payroll can be one of the biggest factors when determining the budget, you can maximize the most by utilizing as many entry-level personnel as possible. Also keep in mind, if you are functioning as your own HR department, you need to set up some kind of formalized review and interview process. The sooner you do this, the faster you will get crewed up.

As far as attracting experienced talent goes, setting up a booth at one of the major game developer conferences is a great strategy (Game Developer's Conference, E3, Austin Game Developer's Conference, to list a few). Keep in mind, that the more experience and talent a person possesses, the bigger the salary he or she will want. These are the people, though, that you will hire to be department leads, and they will be the ones that take you to a successful final product.

Either way, once a good-sized stack of perspective applicants has been decided upon (usually by screening out people using phone interviews), it's time to set up some formal interviews. Some of the important topics to cover in the interview are: gaps in employment, multiple jobs in a short period of time, references, responsibilities at the last position, and future goals of the applicant. Also, it's a good idea to include as many members of the department that the person is interviewing for in the interview. Once the interview is over, the department can then discuss how they feel the person would fit in with them (sometimes called the "culture" of the workplace) and whether the producer should extend a job offer to the applicant.

The hiring process can be a long one—especially if you need a lot of specialized and experienced personnel. When you are all crewed up, the last thing you need is fast turnover (people quitting/getting fired). This problem can be prevented by implementing some great programs at the studio designed to retain personnel. In addition to the obvious perks (benefits and great environment), some other things you can institute around the studio include the following: on-site gym, kitchen with coffee bar/snacks, game room (useful for competitive research and enjoying downtime), and cross-training (engineers always enjoy learning about the art side of the house and vice versa). These things help you keep a solid and happy studio functioning.

Once the task of hiring the development team is finished and leads for each department have been identified, it's time for a chain of communication to be established.

2.3 Learning to Scrum

"Scrum" is the basic terminology used for Agile Software Development practices. There are tons of books about the topic— as well as some great Web sites—but the one I recommend is *Agile Software Development with SCRUM* by Ken Schwaber and Mike Beedle (Prentice Hall, 2001). Basically, the fundamental practice of a scrum is to develop a game bit by bit, reviewing the current component in a meeting environment, then moving on to the next step in development through team consensus. It is the regular meetings of directors, producers, and leads that constitute scrumming ("scrum" is a rugby term for when all the players huddle up on the field to continue play).

One of the most valuable things to learn when beginning the practice of Agile development is to not go into the realm of meeting overload! Regular production meetings are extremely important (especially in the beginning of development) and should be of the highest priority on the schedule, but many times a producer can schedule too many meetings and leads find themselves constantly off the floor (where the younger, inexperienced developers need them) and in meetings. A great way to avoid this is to assign senior team members who are not the leads to attend the scrums and provide input.

The basic scrum session is made up of a scrum master and representatives of each department engaging in planning and brainstorming. This team typically works on small sets of tasks designed to help the development process for everyone in achievable, but small periods of time called "sprints". Each scrum/sprint builds upon the one completed before it. Soon, these small, manageable tasks get the team on track to turn in another deliverable or reach a scheduled milestone.

Creating a completed, cinematic game like *BioShock* is accomplished with many sprints and milestones. Reproduced by permission of 2K Games. All rights reserved.

The use of Agile development and scrums can create a more focused development cycle, build a team with a higher morale and focus, and implement a simple way for tracking progress. Usually, the scrum is used in conjunction with a typical project management system (such as Microsoft Project) and is one of the fundamental practices of the gaming industry. There are aspects of Agile development that can be especially helpful when initially planning the game, too (in the concept/game plan phase), such as discussing the methodologies by which the development team will work together and support each other. This method is preferable to the old model of "code-like-hell, fix-like-hell".

Other viable approaches to development (there are many) include the practices known as the Iterative (or Incremental) method and the Waterfall (or Cascade) method.

2.4 Iterative and Waterfall Development Models

Sometimes called the "iterate-until-you-drop" method, the Iterative development model is based around the idea of developing a game in small increments, then taking advantage of everything learned/gained when developing subsequent steps. The approach revolves around an initialization step that creates a base version of what is being developed, then an iteration step that involves experimenting with and creating a product based upon a control list of features and tasks that need to be performed. This approach usually involves cross-discipline work that focuses on functionality. The flexibility of this approach makes it quite appealing to development teams, and the use of analysis and measurement help ensure a quality product.

By contrast, the Waterfall development method is very step-driven and methodical. It focuses on the idea of working sequentially through the various stages of development (analysis, design, implementation, testing, integration, and maintenance), then delivering the final product. There are various spin-offs of this model—and most are criticized for the belief that a particular development step can be made perfect before continuing to the next step. The Waterfall method does not allow for implementing later changes to earlier ideas—or at least not doing so with any ease. For these reasons, the Waterfall/Cascade method of development is usually avoided.

Whichever method you determine to suit your production needs will include a great deal of project management.

> **Production Tip**
>
> Learning more about software engineering is as easy as picking up a book that will go into more detail regarding this subject. Check out *Software Engineering: A Practitioner's Approach* by Roger S. Pressman (McGraw-Hill, 2004).

2.5 Project Management

Most producers in the game industry have a background in some sort of project management. This can be as formal as having obtained an MBA or certification through the Project Management Institute (or through Microsoft) or as informal as possessing experience from working on past projects (in or out of the game industry). Either way, chances are good that they will be working with Microsoft Project.

Without getting into the nitty-gritty of Project, the simplest way to understand how it works is to envision the development of your game in what is called a "critical path". This concept is a sort of step-by-step way of looking at creating your game. Because certain steps have to be completed before other steps (called "dependencies"), a chain of tasks must be accomplished and finished before moving on to the next step.

Each step in the critical path can be plotted in the program to incorporate a schedule, keep you on budget, and to allocate resources for each task that is being assigned. In a nutshell, it's an all-in-one program for keeping the project on track—exactly what the program was designed for! Usually, the producers track the progress of development using a project management program such as Project as their primary tool for determining how and when a project is getting off track.

Alternatively, more and more producers are starting to use Microsoft Excel for tracking. Though it does not have the ability to create reports about schedule, resources, and so on, Excel does allow you to keep detailed flowcharts annotated with milestone schedules and dates that deliverables should be finished. Excel is also easier to read for those not acquainted with Project. This ease helps immensely when making reports regarding daily progress (sometimes called "daily delta reports") or discussing the status of production in a studio meeting.

Another way that progress is tracked throughout the development process is the use of online documentation. Most productions use an internal Web site, maintained by the individual departments, that lists the status of current tasks and the progress that is being made (sometimes this is a wiki page, sometimes it is a blog template). This site becomes an important tool by allowing the producer to see what is being accomplished on a daily basis throughout the team. The information extracted from the site usually affects what is going into the daily reporting to the studio and publisher.

The primary goal and concern for every project manager—a producer or director—is to keep the production of the game on schedule and on budget.

2.6 Budgeting

When creating the budget for a project, one primary concern must be kept in mind: the game needs to make a profit! The lower the bottom line, the more likely a publisher is to pick up the title. You probably need to have a schedule in place before finalizing the budget, but if you have the rough schedule, you can usually begin forming the specifics of the budget.

The budget must include every aspect of creating the game, including labor (including outside contract work and any benefits involved with employment), the overhead for maintaining the studio during production, any equipment that will be needed by the development team (computers, other hardware, specialized software, and so on), all fees for the title (licensing), and morale. More often than not, the expense involved with keeping a team in high spirits is one of the areas that bloom out of control—along with feature creep and overly ambitious schedules.

Any time the production team gets into a crunch period (usually right before a milestone is reached and the end of production), it is necessary to foot the bill for many meals, morale trips, and so on to keep the team motivated. As personnel will be working ungodly hours (far more than usual, at any rate), they will be eating a majority of their meals on the job—and on your tab! Creating a more realistic schedule helps alleviate this issue, and this contingency must be factored into the budget.

With a great budget and schedule, great games are created—like Activision's *Call of Duty 4: Modern Warfare*. Reproduced by permission of Activision. All rights reserved.

Sitting down with the directors and producers to form an itemized budget is a tedious but necessary evil. Once a department-by-department budget is created (See the Sample Budget in Appendix A: Extras), the next task is to stay on budget! Again, whether you're using a project management system or a simple spreadsheet to achieve this goal, the closer the team sticks to the budget, the better your relationship with the publisher will be. Ideally, the original budget would be the one to take the team through the entire production phase; realistically, though, there will be contingencies that cannot be completely anticipated. These usually revolve around labor, travel (including attending various conferences), and feature creep. It is an unfortunate reality that, no matter what development model the team utilizes, the budget will have to be revised a few times curing production. Again, to keep in the good graces of the publisher, it is a good idea to stay as close to the original projected budget and schedule as possible.

In addition to *affecting* the budget, the schedule will also be *determined* by the budget. Knowing in advance how much you will have to spend on your game will give you a great idea of how much time you will be able to afford in production.

2.7 Scheduling

Creating a detailed schedule is perhaps the most challenging part of getting the project underway. There will always be tasks that have slipped through the cracks, tasks that take much longer than planned, and dependencies that seem to never get finished so that the team can move on. These must be dealt with on a daily basis. Feature creep is the stuff producers have nightmares about and the bane of any production.

There are several ways to approach the creation of a schedule including the top-down approach, the bottom-up approach, and working with various constraints (time, resources, and money to name a few). Most project management personnel have their own favorite method. One of the most common ways to approach a schedule is to think of the critical path for developing the game. Once you have your chain of tasks and have assigned a duration/period for accomplishing each of these tasks, you will have a basic schedule. Though the production may run for years, it is still necessary to have some kind of idea regarding when each major milestone should be reached. When determining these, get all of the department leads involved. Their experience will ensure that the schedule is realistic and achievable. It will also keep them from casting blame when a milestone suddenly seems unreachable and the team careens into crunch time.

Planning for contingencies will be another necessary task when preparing the final schedule. As the development of a game can occur over a very long period of time, many changes will occur throughout the studio. There will be holidays, personnel changes, vacations, conferences, crunch time (overtime), and training of new employees. There should be a contingency fund set aside for just these occurrences.

Creating a realistic schedule takes time and many meetings, so don't forget to allow for this in the budget. Taking steps during the concept phase to document the scope of work involved with producing the proposed game will help with this. Rely on the experience of the senior team members to accurately gauge the amounts of time involved with producing each of the particular features of the game. A balance between concept and reality will eventually be reached.

At the minimum, an early schedule should have the basics listed with a set date: production, QA, and the Gold Master. Once these major dates have been determined, the production phase can be broken down into the various milestones that must be reached and the lists of criteria that need to be fulfilled before moving on to the next phase.

Once the schedule is finished, the game plan for development is wrapped up and preproduction of the game is officially finished. With the budget, schedule, and concept package firmly in hand, you can now move on into production.

Interview: Warren Spector, Founder, Junction Point Studios

Warren Spector has worked in the game industry for more than twenty years. After six years at Steve Jackson Games and TSR creating pen-and-paper games, Spector spent seven years at Origin Systems producing several addictive games, including *Ultima Underworld: The Stygian Abyss, Ultima Underworld II: Labyrinth of Worlds, System Shock, Ultima VII Part Two: Serpent Isle, Wings of Glory, Bad Blood, Ultima Worlds of Adventure 2: Martian Dreams, CyberMage*, and many more. A brief stint with Looking Glass Technologies was followed by a seven-year association with Ion Storm. After founding Ion Storm's Austin studio in 1997, he directed the development of its genre-bending, award-winning game *Deus Ex*. He later oversaw development of Ion Storm's *Deus Ex: Invisible War*, released in December 2003, and *Thief: Deadly Shadows*, released in June 2004. He left Ion Storm in November 2004 to found Junction Point Studios, Inc., which was acquired by Disney Interactive Studios in July 2007.

Though now a fixture in the electronic gaming world, Spector's gaming roots are in the pen-and-paper game business, where he developed *Toon: The Cartoon Roleplaying Game* (among others) for Steve Jackson Games and at TSR, where he worked on the *Top Secret/SI* Espionage role-playing game, *The Bullwinkle & Rocky Party Roleplaying Game*, and the *Buck Rogers Battle for the 25th Century* board game, to name a few.

In addition to making games, Warren is a published novelist (*The Hollow Earth Affair*, with Richard Merwin, released in 1988), a film reviewer for the the *Austin Chronicle*, an assistant instructor for film and television studies at the University of Texas at Austin, and the author of numerous magazine and newspaper articles. From 2000 to 2002, he served on the Board of Directors of the International Game Developers Association (IDGA) and served as chairman of the IGDA's education committee, forging ties between the game business and academic institutions around the world.

Warren was born and raised in New York City. He graduated from Northwestern University in Evanston, Illinois with a BS in Speech. He received his Master of Arts in Radio-Television-Film from the University of Texas at Austin and remained there to pursue a PhD

Warren Spector

in communications until the video game business lured him away from academia just a dissertation short of a degree. He is a booka-holic, board game fanatic, lover of basketball, and rhythm guitarist for the band "Two-Headed Baby". Warren lives in Austin, Texas with his wife Caroline and far too many animals.

Newman: What aspects of modern/current game development trends have you noticed recently that are taking the industry in the right direction?
Spector: There seems to be a growing market for smaller, less expensive games that at least have a chance of breaking new ground, design-wise. When games cost $10 million, $20 million, and more, it's hard to take a lot of chances. With all the major hardware manufacturers and PC folks offering downloadable games, there are more opportunities for commercially viable, "indie-style" games than ever before. That's kinda cool!

Newman: What, in your opinion, constitutes a "cinematic" game?
Spector: My sarcastic answer is: "A cinematic game is one that doesn't know what it wants to be and therefore shouldn't be made." Basically, while games and movies share many character-istics, it's important—maybe critically important—to recognize, celebrate and exploit the things that make them different. Sure, movies and games can both tell stories structured in superficially similar ways; both can feature actors reciting lines of dialogue; both place a premium on appropriate camera positioning; and so on. But introduce real interactivity into the mix—which only games can do, and therefore *must* do—and the similarities start to look very superficial. There's a gaming truism that the more cinematic you make a game, the less game like it becomes (and vice versa). That's still true today and even if we *can* change it, I'm not sure we should. Games need to borrow the cinematic elements that contribute to a game-like experience, but going too far does violence to both media, I think.

Newman: How has your background in role-playing games helped you with game design?
Spector: Well, the truth is, I had to unlearn a *lot* of things, moving from tabletop role-playing games to electronic games. I mean, you don't appreciate the power of a human game master and players who can improvise freely until you don't have them! But what I did bring with me from the tabletop, face-to-face game world was an appreciation for the intelligence and improvisa-tional abilities of players. They really *do* want to direct their own, unique experiences, and electronic games that "fake" interactivity (keeping players on rails, forcing them down a linear path)—those games are inevitably going to be inferior to games that truly

empower players to make their own, unique choices—and deal with the consequences of those choices.

Newman: Another aspect of gaming that has improved is the storytelling. Has the game writing standard improved in your opinion and how has it affected the gamer?

Spector: I guess game writing has gotten somewhat better over the years. But, fundamentally, players play games to, you know, *play*. They don't play games to read a bunch of text or wait around while a virtual character pontificates for hours. If game developers had any idea how to make conversation as dynamic and interactive as we make the more active, visceral aspects of our games, we'd really be on to something. So far, I'm not real impressed with the progress we've made on that front. Frankly, if I knew how to solve what I call "the conversation problem," I'd do it! Given the limits of our conversation tools, I think the best we can hope for is that game writers will learn a lesson from screenwriters—those guys are masters, absolute masters, of brevity. Read a movie script and marvel at how much emotion and character can be crammed into a word or two; a gesture; a look. It's incredible. Game writers have to write a *whole* lot less, if I can over-generalize a bit!

Newman: Over the years, you've been involved with quite a few successful games—the *Ultima* series and *Deus Ex* come quickly to mind. What characteristics mark a great franchise title?

Spector: I wish I knew! There's a fair amount of bottled lightning involved! Having said that, I *think* it probably has to do with subject matter—either on the surface or as subtext—that people really care about. Your game has to be about something bigger than the minute-to-minute actions of the player. I also think you need a compelling central character. And you need a world that's so well thought out, so well realized, that people can believe they're really there. And, of course, the game play has to be rock-solid and innovative—we're still a novelty-driven medium, more than a content-driven one. If you're not offering players something they haven't seen before, you have a real uphill battle.

Newman: Since consoles have added the ability for online gaming, the social aspects of being a gamer have improved considerably. How much impact does online content have upon the success of a game today?

Spector: No idea. I've only worked on one game that had any online aspect—the *Deus Ex* Game of the Year Edition shipped with a competitive multiplayer mode that we did as more of an experiment than anything else. I wanted to see if our unique avatar/unique experience concept would translate to a different multiplayer experience than people were used to. I think it worked, for what it's worth, though I don't think many people tried it! Anyway, it's certainly true that online aspects are an important bullet point on the back of a game box, and there are clearly lots of people who want a social experience as they play. I just hope that doesn't supplant the single-player experience, which has its own pleasures and (still untapped) potential.

Newman: When Origin closed up shop in Austin, it seemed that the talent you had gathered there moved on to form the core for quite a few new studios. What "lessons learned" did you consider when you formed your new studio, Junction Point?

Spector: I learned a ton from the Origin and Ion Storm experiences—a book's worth! I think I came to appreciate how important team fit was to success. And it's critical to have team members and publishing partners who believe in your mission. Without a positive culture and committed collaborators, you can't succeed. That's probably the most important thing I tried to bear in mind when I started Junction Point.

Newman: Now that J.P. is affiliated with Disney—most known, of course, for films—has the game development style of the studio become more cinematic? What great practices has the studio added from Disney?

Spector: I don't know that we've become "more cinematic" in our thinking. I mean, if you check out our Web site you'll find an abridged version of our mission statement. (The longer version can be found on my blog site: http://junctionpoint.wordpress.com/) That mission hasn't changed at all since we became part of Disney. In fact, I've always made a point of reminding people I work with—including Disney, now—that if they don't want games like the ones I talk about in the mission statement, we probably shouldn't work together! Having said that, we're all psyched about how open the guys at Disney, on the film side, have been about sharing their expertise with us. I mean, there are ways in which games and movies are similar, and collaboration can make both media stronger. Working with the Disney film guys has already been an education for me and I don't see that changing—gotta keep learning!

Newman: What advice would you give a young producer/director just getting into the game development industry?

Spector: Well, get it out of your head that you're going to start as a producer or director, for starters! Figure out where you can really make an impact in the trenches of game development. You need to prove yourself as a designer or artist or programmer or audio person or tester or *something* before you even think about moving into a larger creative or management role. Remember, always, that ideas are the easy part of game development—execution is insanely hard. Until you've been through it a few times, you can't even imagine! So learn as much as you can about how games are made; figure out what aspect of game development you love— what you're really, really good at (it's an ultra-competitive business); find developers or publishers who make the kind of game you love to play, and don't give up until you get your foot in the door. On a somewhat related note, if you're in school, stay there. A broad-based education will serve you well in this business.

3

PRODUCTION IN THE GAME INDUSTRY

Though this is by no means an exhaustive look into the world of producing a video game, this chapter will give you an idea of just what is involved with game development. Part 4 of this book covers some of these topics in more detail—mostly geared towards the production of an "independent" game. In this primer, we take a more succinct look at the various elements involved with getting production up and rolling.

One of the first major decisions that you will make as a director/ producer is what types of technology will be used in designing and programming your title. Although some areas of game dev have almost standardized tools (for instance, it is almost an inevitability that animators will be using 3ds Max and Maya), the choices of

Creating a game like Midway's *Blacksite: Area 51* means using a lot of software and tools. Reproduced by permission of Midway Games. All rights reserved.

game engines and middleware are growing on an almost daily basis. Factors that determine which tools you will use include the needs of the engineers, the costs of licensing and using certain software, and the platforms the game will be played on.

3.1   Technology and Tools

Early on—probably during designing the game concept and design document—the technical leads will evaluate the game and the requirements needed to accomplish development. These decisions will be made based on the budget (some software can carry a pretty high licensing fee), the level of graphics and functionality desired, and the knowledge base of the team. Sometimes, the team is chosen after the tools have been determined and hiring is based upon experience with these tools.

Either way, the major areas of software include game engines, AI systems (artificial intelligence), necessary middleware (software designed to work with another existing program), and physics systems. All of these needs will have to be addressed—and you can actually get middleware programs for most of these areas (meaning that you can get second-party-developed software to handle specific needs rather than licensing expensive programs from the developer of your game engine). The area of middleware is huge in the game industry right now and is a huge source of employment for engineers/programmers.

Of course, some developers make the decision to create their own proprietary technology for game creation. Though this can add considerable time to the project, the studio will own the program and will not have to shell out any money for licensing. There is also the added benefit of being able to sell your engine to other developers for income. Either way, once the software package has been determined, the tech leads will create a pipeline or workflow for the game.

The pipeline is basically the path that the team takes regarding the creation, programming, and implementing of individual game assets. Because most items in a game must be compiled or converted to fit the programming needs of the game, it's important to establish this workflow early. Some of the things to identify when constructing this pipeline are the critical path for getting the work done, the tracking system for monitoring production and bugs, and any risks that could affect production.

Once the tools are in place and the pipeline is established, the team can move on to the individual development requirements and workflow needed for the design, art, and engineering departments.

Development Tip

A great way to familiarize yourself with a game engine is to get one! You can pick up the Torque game engine from Garage Games or the XNA game engine from Microsoft for a very low price. Also, many of the programs involved with game development have free trial versions that you can download for free. Working on mods for other games is another great way to learn about this area as well.

3.2 Design Production

Early in the process, you must choose the tools and middleware that will best serve the programming needs of your game. As mentioned earlier, the tools needed to support the actual game design will be evident in the choices of functionality present in your game. Some of the factors in the design that will require technology/tool choices include sound design, artificial intelligence, and physics. Another factor influencing your choice of game engine and middleware should be the ability to make changes easily.

Once the design team has begun the development process, the need to change the functionality within the game and test the existing features will become quite evident. The ability to make changes and add additional functionality should be one of the deciding factors when choosing your software for development.

Some of the game elements to be considered when choosing software includes the use of speech, use of game controls, and any detailed data that must be monitored during game play (such as scoring, levels, and so on). The ability to iterate and change these functions during development should be a deciding factor when choosing a game engine and middleware. Though redesigns should be kept at a minimum, they are almost an inevitability and the software must allow for this.

Also, the feedback that the design team receives from the QA department will become an important tool for designing subsequent builds on the game and ensuring that all functionality is on point. The basic workflow of the design team involves implementing features, testing features, and then making appropriate changes to the builds to accommodate this information (all to be approved by the directors/producers).

3.3 Art Production

On the art side of the house, the workflow goes a bit differently. Once the basic concept art has been approved and the team is in alignment with the overall artistic vision and look of the game (a lengthy process that involves creative meetings focusing on the script, production, and goals of the game), the art team begins the lengthy process of creating art assets within the game. These assets can be everything from the locations and buildings to the individual characters, props, and vehicles used throughout the game. Often, the list of assets can be so long that much of this work is outsourced to external parties.

An example of concept art from *Lost Planet: Extreme Condition*. Reproduced by permission of Capcom U.S.A., Inc. All rights reserved.

Typically, the art team has sets of deadlines for "deliverables" (individual items) and individual artists/animators has specific assets assigned to them. It's usually a good idea to assign a specific animator or artist to each character to ensure continuity throughout the game. As the art team creates more and more assets, they begin working closely with the engineering team to ensure that the assets can be integrated into the game.

Some of the more prevalent programs in the art department include Adobe Photoshop, Autodesk Maya, and Autodesk 3ds Max. There are other 3D modeling programs, as well as painting programs used for coloring and applying textures, that are more specialized and available as well, though finding artists that specialize in them may be more difficult.

3.4   Engineering Production

The engineering team is responsible for researching and coding everything into the actual game, as well as debugging any problems that occur. As they receive assets, they code and engineer them into the game using the tools and software available.

Every time the code changes within the game, a new build is essentially created. Depending on the schedule and budget you have in place, new builds can be made available on a daily, weekly, or milestone basis. Every new build means more debugging and another pass through the QA department. It is the smooth operation of these cycles that gets the game through development and into publishing.

It is important to also take into consideration the use of revision (or version) control system software. This is just one of the ways you can track changes to code within the game, as well as manage it. You can even use this software to keep multiple versions of the game archived as they are created. Best of all, if something is working you can see who made the changes to it, as well as allow multiple people to work with/from the same code.

There are literally hundreds of choices in software, depending on the engineering needs of the game. At the very least, you should address all the various sections of the programming team (AI, graphics engine, game flow, network, database, user interface, tools, installation, and sound)—this is best done by speaking with the technical leads for the department. Because the technical side of the house becomes even more complicated when you begin to discuss the game's platform (or the use of cross-platform development) and the various programming elements of the game (including the programming language, libraries, debug systems, and profilers), it's best to let your tech leads guide your way.

Making a game geared to a single console, like *Halo 3*, definitely has its advantages. Copyright © Bungie LLC and/or its suppliers. All rights reserved.

Different systems have different costs and considerations involved with them—and some are easier to acquire/use than others. Some of the more common choices today for programmers include OpenGL, Microsoft Visual C++, and Microsoft's

XNA/DirectX programs. There are also specialized programs that focus on artificial intelligence and on physics, as well as middleware that helps implement functionality between the programs being used. Most of these choices will of course be based upon the game engine that you use.

Communication between the art, design, and engineering teams is essential for the production to remain on schedule (yes, everyone will actually have to use the wiki/online collaboration tools and attend assigned meetings). All departments should take time testing new levels as well—everyone can make suggestions and improvements in the game play. The individual teams should be in contact with the QA department as well to track bugs and correct them as they occur.

3.5   The Team

In addition to the personnel who typically run a studio (management)—this would include the creative director, studio head, and the administrative personnel—there are four general areas of employment in the game industry: art, design, programming, and testing. Testing will be discussed later this chapter; first, let's take a look at the other three areas.

The art department is usually made up of character artists, animators, background artists (sometimes called "digital matte painters"), and sometimes texture artists, though most character artists are also skilled at texture work. When the individual assets for the game have been dealt out to the various artists in the departments, there is typically a lead that is in charge of making sure that each artist pulls his/her weight and turns in assets on time.

The design team includes level/mission designers who report to a lead as well. Though the design team is involved with the production process early in the basic game design plan (this includes designing the locations of obstacles, goals, and props throughout the game), designers are also expected to be able to modify levels and continue designing throughout the production process. Any changes made to the basic design require the designers to be able to adjust the level plans accordingly.

The programming team involves all the personnel assigned to the various coding tasks associated with making the game. Every tool or program that's involved in creating your title will require a mini-team of programmers to work with it—this includes the game engine, all middleware, graphics, artificial intelligence, and any specialized programs that will be involved. The programmers also report to a lead that then reports to the technical director.

In addition to the studio directors (creative and technical), there are also a number of producers involved with managing the various teams and logistics for developing the game. The producers are responsible for making sure that the teams are working on schedule and budget, as well as reporting progress to the studio. Producers come from all aspects of game development, but a general knowledge of the tools being used (coupled with a strong project management background) is a must. Producers come in quite a few varieties including associate producers, assistant producers, line producers, and full-blown producers (we will discuss this aspect more and in great detail in Chapter 8 of this book). Other details that must be familiar to the producer include licensing and negotiation, testing, and localization.

There are also personnel who will be involved with creating the music, sound effects, and recording the voice over for the game. Sometimes the music is outsourced to local music producers/composers, but having an internal composer capable of writing and recording music is a definite plus for the production.

3.6   Sound Design

Though video games are thought of as a visual medium, the truth is that one of the most important characteristics of a successful title is the sound design. Sound designers usually have a background in studio engineering, music production, and composition. Deciding upon the right sound designer for your project rests entirely on the style of music you want for the game. Will it be an electronic-based soundtrack or a traditional symphonic score? Once you know the type of soundtrack you want, you can then select an appropriate composer/designer.

The symphonic score by Jeremy Soule contributes immensely to the cinematic production value of Bethesda's *Elder Scrolls IV: Oblivion.* The Elder Scrolls IV: Oblivion® © 2006 Bethesda Softworks LLC, a ZeniMax Media company. All rights reserved.

It also important to know the types of audio tools the sound designers are familiar with. With many different options available on the market (Pro Tools, Soundforge, Propellerhead Reason, Cakewalk, among others), you can and should make sure that you have the appropriate programs on hand for that designer.

In addition to the music involved with the game, the sound design team is also skilled in sampling and designing sound effects. Every individual sound used in the game—everything from the sounds of walking/running to gunshots to animal sounds—must be created or recorded by the sound design team. In addition to obtaining sounds the traditional way (recording them), there are also sound effect libraries available for licensing. Most of these are quite reasonable—and even more cost-effective when you consider the logistics of recording some sound effects.

Much like the art department, the sound design team will have a laundry list of assets that must be acquired: music and songs, cut-scene scores, ambient sound and music, sound effects, and "stingers" (brief musical trills that punctuate a defeat, victory, or achievement), to name a few. It is important for these assets to be named and filed appropriately as well, so organization skills can be a factor when making a choice.

A great way to approach the sound design of a game is to use "temp tracks" in development—standard tracks extracted from other musical works that are temporarily used in the game to illustrate the type of music desired for that portion of game play. Once the music styles match the desired mood and scope of the game, you can then work on getting original music composed in the vein of the temp tracks. This approach can also be used with stock sound effects.

Often, the sound design team is also in charge of recording any voiceover used in the game, though the use of external sound studios is also a viable route.

3.7 Motion Capture and Voiceover

Before going into a voiceover session, make sure that the dialogue is reasonably set within the script. Though a little improvisation may occur during recording, the bulk of the dialogue should be written in stone. Before going to the studio, the producer should sit down with that script and make direction and technical notes. These notes should include the names that will be assigned to each sound file (this step helps with importing the audio into the game), as well as any key elements relevant to the recording (such as "character is very angry").

Every character within the game must have an actor for the voiceover work. If your sound designer has no background in voiceovers, it may be wise to directly involve a producer or external sound engineer when recording as well. Finding the talent needed for the characters is usually the most difficult step. The use of an outside casting director is usually recommended for filling the roles (see the chapter in this book about casting). As the voiceover work is being recorded, it is necessary to remember the context of the lines being read, so that the actor can be directed to use the appropriate level of emotion or concern when recording. Once all sounds and music have been generated and archived with appropriate file names, the game will wait for audio postproduction.

When creating file names for the various elements you are recording, it is also important to remember that you may be localizing the game in multiple languages. Make sure to annotate the files with the appropriate locale in the name. In addition to working outside the studio for the voiceover work, there will also be the use of a motion capture studio in most game productions.

Though some studios do have an on-site motion capture studio (or at least an area devoted to it), the typical practice is to outsource the motion capture work. Generally, the producers hire actors with motion capture (mo-cap) experience, work with them to outline the general movements of the characters they will be portraying, then accompany them to the mo-cap studio to do the actual work. Again, directing techniques are needed to get the appropriate character traits out of each bit of capture (cinematic directing techniques will be discussed thoroughly in Part 2 of this book). Though the game may have many characters, it is not uncommon to use only a couple of actors for all the various roles. This is why it is important to let the actor know the particular character they are portraying in each move and the context of the action they are performing.

Whether you are using professional motion capture actors, general actors, or just a couple people from the studio, it is important to allow for the mo-cap work in the budget, as well as the time needed to translate the information from the session into the game.

Extensive use of motion capture makes for ultra-realistic movement in Ubisoft's game *Assassin's Creed*. Reproduced by permission of UbiSoft. All rights reserved.

3.8   Testing and Quality Assurance

The final team you will deal with during production is the QA department. Though this area is usually reserved for people who are entering the industry at the ground level (sometimes the QA personnel are even gamers with little-to-no game development experience), make sure that there are experienced QA leads here and a well-seasoned QA manager. The QA team tracks bugs throughout the game development process and works with the programming department to fix these bugs, so it's important that this department is well-trained and well-equipped to handle their job. Some of the elements that the QA team look at include the functionality of the game, the cohesion of the story, the game's interface, and the compatibility of the game with the intended hardware to be played on—and, most importantly, the bugs themselves!

The QA manager is responsible for managing the testing team, reporting bugs to the producers, and tracking the various builds of the game to make sure they are on point. This team can be utilized in-house as part of the game studio, or the entire QA process can be outsourced to an external studio or team. With the availability of high-quality bug tracking software, though, it is advisable to attempt to keep the team within the studio.

Though hiring a QA department costs money, this cost can be less than that of outsourcing the work. Factors that will influence your decision regarding the QA department include the availability of skilled testers, the game's overall budget, and the amount of time allowed for Alpha and Beta testing in the schedule. Having the department in-house will speed up the testing process—also, the studio will now have the software and department in place for the next project, so you won't have to purchase testing software again. Having the team on-site also allows for closer collaboration between QA and the producers. This can have a positive impact on your schedule and managing payments to contractors. Also, many game designers believe that keep young, fresh game testers on the payroll is an easy way to keep a game cutting-edge with current technology and trends.

However, if there simply is a shortage of local talent for game testing—the pay for this department is usually not high enough to entice people to move—it may become necessary to outsource this work. Using an established testing firm means getting a level of professionalism that you may not have had in your own studio, as well as not spending money regarding the overhead of housing another department.

The QA team also gets the final crack at the Gold Master at the end of production. This is the final round of testing that will

Development Tip

Are you interested in being a game tester? Download a trial version of TechExcel DevTrack (http://www.techexcel.com) or TestTrack Pro from Seapine software (http://www.seapine.com) and get a leg up on the competition.

determine whether the game is ready to ship to the publisher. Though most of the responsibility of the QA department falls under the QA manager (sometimes referred to as only a lead), it is also the duty of the producers to make sure that bugs are being tracked and resolved (or closed).

Letting a backlog of bugs get out of hand is one of the quickest ways to get a game off schedule. Bugs should be addressed as early as possible when discovered so that the programmers will still be familiar with that code that was generated. A great way to track bugs is to make sure that all builds include a level of accountability. If a new build breaks when played, it will be easy to see what assets were introduced in that version of the game— as well as what probably caused the problem.

Some of the perks of getting a game properly through a long-term QA process include implementing a quick release worldwide (as localizing issues will have been addressed), preventing piracy by implementing copy protection, and getting a quick thumbs-up from console manufacturers.

Interview: Ray Pena, Senior Animator, Spacetime Studios

Ray Pena has more than ten years of experience in games and film. He has worked as an animator on the *Turok* video game series and was the art director on *The Red Star* game based on the award-winning comic series, while at Acclaim. Other works include animation on *The Ant Bully* and *Everyone's Hero* feature films. Ray also worked on *Area 51:Blacksite* for Midway. He's done work for Disney and Nickelodeon for television shows including *Jimmy Neutron: Boy Genius*.

Newman: As an animator, you are in a position to work in both the game and film industries. Describe the challenges of keeping up with both communities and how you stay on top of technology.

Pena: Well, knowing a lot of folks in both industries helps me keep up with what's being worked on and any films or games that are the buzz in either community. I'm a member of a few Google Groups that include game and film animators/crew. I also peruse the forums often to see what the latest is in software, animation and modeling techniques, and so on. There's so much to keep up with, though, that it's difficult to be well versed in all aspects of 3D art. That's why I focused on animation.

Newman: Have you worked on an animated film before? If so, what lessons learned/good practices did you bring with you to the game industry?

Pena: Yes. Planning is the single most important lesson I learned from film. Before, I always did what I thought looked cool and that seemed to work quite often. In film, my acting choices weren't always the best. So I sketched a lot, blocked in my anims pose to pose in a stepped key method, then I submitted that. I had to approach it as key drawings. It felt slow at the beginning of the process, but it sure did make life easier when changes were requested or the director simply pointed me in the right direction. Nowadays, I always do sketches for my animations and get a feel for what others around me think about it. It's always good to get opinions from other animators or just anyone before, during and after the creation of your animation. I tend to think more in depth of what a character's purpose is as well. I consider what their motivation is, what their history may be. Are they evil? Do they have good intentions? Are they quick or slow? Heavy or light? Male or female? Clumsy or agile? Right-handed or left-handed? Married, single or divorced? Do they have a hearing problem?

Newman: What programs/software would you recommend that a recent animation graduate in the game industry master?
Pena: It's not the software that makes a good animator. It's about knowing the principles of animation and nuances of movement in bringing characters and objects to life. But, that said, the industry standards in 3D animation are 3ds Max and Maya. If you know one program, you pretty much know them all. It's just about finding the buttons at that point.

Newman: Typically, a day on the job for you would involve…
Pena: Animating. Lots of animating. I've been working on some alien creatures lately, so studying insects and sea life is always included. I'm always taking a look at videos online or on DVD of anything that could inspire me. The research is never done, it seems.

Newman: Describe your workflow; where does your work come from and where do you hand it off?
Pena: The ideas usually start from the design team, the folks who create the gameplay and fiction of the game. That is described to the concept artists. Once they are happy with sketches, color studies, and so on, they hand everything off to the modelers/texture artists. I like to keep up with what's going on in these early steps so that I can start getting my head around what motivates these characters.

Newman: In most cases, do animators create the actual artistic look of the characters, vehicles, and similar items that they are creating, or is there usually an artist involved?
Pena: I like to throw in my two cents occasionally, but usually I let the concept artists do their job. They've always been open to input from us. I usually look at it from an animation perspective,

obviously. Concerns I sometimes have are something like, are these arms worth having on the character if they're useless? Is this weapon too big for this specific character?

Newman: Describe the creative process involved with meeting the overall artistic vision for the project when creating original animation.

Pena: The animators will always have an initial meeting with the lead designer, lead concept artist, and art director to discuss a character. We talk about every animation for that character and what direction we want to take it. Of course, there will always be differing opinions, but it's great to come to a consensus and a well thought out idea. I usually then go back to my office and sketch as much as possible to nail down key poses and arcs.

Newman: Artists are known for their passionate opinions concerning their own art. How do you handle a clash in opinion when you feel an asset needs to go in a different direction?

Pena: I'm always open to criticism. That's one thing every artist needs to learn to deal with early on. I don't always agree with criticism of my work, but I love talking about finding a common direction that could be better than my opinion and the others I'm working with.

Newman: Because you are a senior animator, a team of additional animators work in your department with you. How do you communicate a game plan to the team for a particular sprint/milestone? How do you keep them focused?

Pena: We usually try to stick to one animator per character. That way they are able to keep it consistent in all of its motions. Seeing a character come together in the game is always very satisfying. I think that's always a lot of motivation for any animator. There will always be bumps along the way. The anims sometimes don't match up well with one another or the milestone may just be too long to keep focus, but it's great to see the characters come to life. That always gives me a boost of excitement.

Newman: What advice would you give an animator just getting into the job market?

Pena: Work hard! Nothing will be given to you. To get ahead, you have to be thinking ahead of everyone else. Study animated films, live action films, animals, people and anything that moves. Inspiration will always be around you. Take acting classes. I've been to a few workshops. It's scary sometimes, but very fun too. And of course, put all of that to use. Study with a purpose. Know why you're looking at how an arm swings during a walk cycle or how most things will naturally move in some sort of arc. Networking is very important as well. Always be good to everyone around you. You never know who may be your boss someday.

4

POSTPRODUCTION

Unlike the film industry (where months of editing, color correction, and releasing the film is involved), postproduction in the game industry is a relatively short period (when compared to the actual production phase, anyway). The game, for all practical purposes, is pretty much finished at this point. Postproduction in the video game industry is more about wrapping up the production and preparing for the next project. There are also some inescapable necessities that must be performed at the end of the production cycle to ensure that your product will be available throughout the world, that it will sell, and that you will be in a position to launch your next title—such as setting up a customer support network and being prepared to code and create any necessary patches to your finished game.

Games like Bungie Studio's *Halo 3* take advantage of Beta testing with gamers all over the world to make sure the game is ready for release. Copyright © Bungie LLC and/or its suppliers. All rights reserved.

The beginning of postproduction is usually marked by the release of the Gold Master; this is the final version of the game that will be mass produced by the publisher. The Gold Master is the game after it has made it through the approval processes of the studio, the console manufacturers, and the publisher during code release. Once it is out the door, the studio can begin preparing for the next title to be produced.

4.1   Code Release and Gold Master

Think of this stage as quality control. At this point all the minor/major bugs involved with game play have been corrected, but the game must make it through the QA department's final set of checks and validation before the game can be sent on to the publisher. Though this is usually not a terribly long process (unless you've rushed to the Gold Master because of an unreasonable milestone schedule), it must be included in the schedule —usually a couple weeks—it can be an extremely involved process. Depending on the number of platforms the game will be released on and how many localizations are initially being prepared, each version of the game must go through stringent tests in every area. Once the QA department has given the game the thumbs-up, it can then be sent to be replicated. This is called "code release".

Once the studio acknowledges that the game is ready and it has made it through the code release process, the actual game then is sent for review by the publisher. Chances are good that the game you were developing will be played on one or more consoles; as a result, you will also have to submit the Gold Master to the console's manufacturer for approval as well. In addition to getting approval at these locations, there will also have to be local tests of the game in the various areas in which it will be released to make sure that the game is relevant in the areas it is being released.

4.2   Builds and Localization

Though builds are happening throughout the production process, it's helpful to think of builds in the overall sense of the game. A "build" is basically a version of the game at any point in the production process. Though there are several different approaches to scheduling builds into the production process, it's important to remember that there are a couple builds that will be of huge importance: the Alpha build (which will be the first really playable version of the game), the Beta build (the version that will be tested for final bugs and playability), and the Gold Master.

Localizing a game like *Lost Planet* for multiple countries can take a lot of time and money. Reproduced by permission of Capcom U.S.A., Inc. All rights reserved.

When the game development process reaches its peak at Beta testing, new builds are created on an almost daily basis. Basically, every time a new function, asset, or similar element is added to the game, a new build has just been made. Producers usually track the additions that have been made to each build in a daily report (or build notes) that's made available to the team through the use of version control software. This report is important to the QA department, as they must test all the additions to the title. Usually they do this on a scheduled basis, rather than attempting to keep up with the production team on a day-to-day basis (and because the testing process can be long); they usually run a build for a few days, then move on to the newest build to hit the deck. This means that only every third or fourth build is actually tested—and these are primarily the builds that involve changes in the code. Because the addition of art is not a huge change to the last build, most of these builds won't be immediately tested.

Another set of important builds to consider are those that are created for countries outside of the United States. The process of creating foreign versions of the game is known as "localization". When planned for in advance, localization can be a smooth final step in the production process. This advance planning is usually accomplished by preparing code that will be easily adapted into the foreign versions, organizing assets into easily found directories, and including themes and stories that can be easily translated to other cultures. There must also be an allowance made for creating foreign-language manuals, cover design, and so on.

If the budget for your title is large, chances are good that the localized versions of the game will be released at the same time as the domestic version; however, if you are on a limited budget and schedule, or if you are an independent developer, the different foreign versions will slowly trickle in as they are created. Either way, keep in mind that these versions of the game will be treated just like your original Gold Master; they must be submitted to the publisher and console manufacturers for approval.

There is also the issue of cross-platform development; if you have made the decision to release the game on several consoles and/or the PC, you will have to track every build and version for each of these platforms. This can mean a lot of work in getting to a final Gold Master for every platform you are developing on.

Once the Gold Master is out the door, the public relations (PR) machine will swing into motion.

4.3 Marketing and PR

Long before the game ever touches the shelves, the marketing department will have already put the wheels in motion to create a buzz around the title. The relationship between the game producers and the public relations department usually begins in preproduction! Once the concept is approved and the schedule for production is created, the marketing department will want tentative dates for a demo and completed game shipment so they can plan the marketing campaign for the title.

Games like Ubisoft's *Tom Clancy's Rainbow Six: Vegas 2* start the PR campaign rolling long before the game's actual release. Reproduced by permission of UbiSoft. All rights reserved.

Ideally, the marketing department would simply accept the product from the developer and run with it; however, as most public relations departments have launched many titles, they usually have some great ideas regarding how to make your game more appealing to the game community. These ideas will pop up in the form of requests during the production process. If this happens, it's important to let the department know the impact that adding these items will have on the schedule—this is one of the biggest reasons for developers going over their budget and schedule. It's usually a great idea to make sure the marketing department knows the schedule revolving around important milestones; this knowledge will keep them from making demands on the production team during what will already be extremely busy periods.

During production, as key (or dramatic) art assets are created for the game, it's a great idea to get these to marketing for use in the game manuals and cover art. A failure to do so will usually have them hounding you at some point for these items—they don't want to be the department that holds up the release of the game due to a lack of a manual and box. Work on written documentation for the game should begin as early into production as possible. Sometimes a strategy guide is also in the works for the game, so the amount of hounding you will receive for screenshots, a walkthrough, and similar materials will be enormous!

Besides the actual items needed for the release of the game, the PR/marketing team is also responsible for getting word out to the press about the game. Thus, time must be allotted in the final months of production for press interviews, tradeshows, online previews, and similar events related to your game. When done properly, the game market will be thoroughly saturated with information regarding the title long before the game hits the shelves. Another thing that must happen long before the game's release is to submit the title for a rating.

4.4 Rating Systems, Demos, and Guides

Much like in the film industry, for games to be sold through certain retailers (or for the major console manufacturers), games must be submitted to a group of panelists that review the material for content and then assign a rating to it. In the United States, this group is known as the Entertainment Software Rating Board (ESRB). There are several other important rating boards in the world for localized versions, such as the Pan European Game Information board (PEGI) for a majority of the European countries, the Unterhaltungssoftware Selbstkontrolle (USK) in Germany, and the Computer Entertainment Rating Organization (CERO) who rates the games released for Japan.

Each of these organizations has a set of criteria for each type of rating it offers. Most of these criteria are based around the content of the games, including sexual themes, drug use, violence, profanity, and adult content (anything to do with alcohol, inappropriate social behavior, and gambling). Though ratings boards do nothing to limit the content you include in your game, they enforce the guidelines for rating and give you the most appropriate mark. These ratings must be included even in a demo of the game, so it is extremely important to adhere to the projected rating of the game immediately from the concept phase. You should also take into consideration costs associated with applying for a rating—these can sometimes be substantial fees and should be in the budget.

The rating assigned to the game determines the marketing strategy associated with that game, such as the times that commercials will air on television, and what kind of art can be displayed in magazines and other print. The rating will also ensure that your product does not fall into the wrong hands and that children are unnecessarily exposed to content that is inappropriate for them. Though most countries do follow the recommendations of their appropriate board, some locales are none too friendly to extreme, adult-oriented material. As a result, the game may actually be banned in that country. Developers must adhere to the standards of gaming in the countries they are marketing to if they intend to get their product to the shelves.

Another key factor to a successful game release is going to be the accessibility to a playable demo. Usually, this demo is a step further down the development line than the original demo used to pitch the game or the one that was shown at early game conventions and tradeshows. Typically, the downloadable demo is an example of what will be in the finished game, accompanied by a trailer of some sort. This can be one of the cut-scenes contained within the game or a special cut-scene that was designed for use in selling the product. Ideally, this will be made available to the public just prior to the game's release.

Another great item to have in place at the onset of sales is a strategy guide. This is especially true if the game you have created is a particularly difficult one. Nothing kills the longevity of a title in a player's console than an overly frustrating game. In addition to giving the player helpful clues and a walkthrough for the game, the presence of the book on the shelf helps generate awareness for the game and can create a whole new avenue of revenue for the title.

Games like 2K's *BioShock* are often released simultaneously with a strategy guide. Reproduced by permission of 2K Games. All rights reserved.

Perhaps the biggest role of postproduction in the game industry, though, revolves around the practice of archiving your title.

4.5   Archiving

Once the entire development process is over—all the localized versions are finished, the games and guides are in the stores, and the marketing campaign is in full swing—the production team will now prepare the game for archiving. This stage usually involves performing a lengthy postmortem, documenting all the lessons learned during the production process, and creating a closing kit for the game.

The "postmortem" is basically a final set of meetings with each of the departments to discuss all the things that went right and wrong during the production cycle. Every team member is given the opportunity to speak and weight is given to every item mentioned. Doing this will bring a sense of finality to the project (especially important if many of the people involved with production will be leaving the studio to pursue other projects) and will give permanent personnel working for your studio a great sense of the work culture and ethic of the studio.

Notes should be taken during the postmortem process and then eventually refined into a document that lists the best practices that have been identified and proven to work, as well as the lessons learned, which tend to be the things that didn't quite work. This document will be a major asset when you're planning your next project and will help you with some of the major decisions involved with scheduling, budgeting, and planning. Don't ignore your lessons learned! When you start developing your next title, you will want to revisit this document and prevent your team from making the same mistakes again. Once this has been performed, the closing kit will be assembled.

The "closing kit" is the archived version of the game to be kept for possible future rerelease. All the game's assets, code, and documents associated with production are organized and filed for later use. If you have made several versions of the game (localizations), this will mean several archived closing kits. These kits must be kept accessible, though—down the line, it may become necessary to create fixes for certain areas of the game (or add-on content or modules may be developed) and these will need to be added to the main kit at some point.

The full closing kit is made up of the individual localization kits (each version of the game made) and the localization kits include a translation kit. The translation kit is the folder that contains every item and asset that was translated into the localized version. In addition to the technical aspects of the game's

Development Tip

Publishing your game's postmortem is a great way to contribute to the game development community and get some great PR. Magazines like *Game Developer* and *Game Informer* publish postmortems, as well as Web sites like Gamasutra.

production, you also want to make sure that all marketing items associated with the game's release are also included. This means getting the actual box art and game documentation (manuals and the like) into the kit. The marketing folder in the kit can also contain the original demo and screenshots that were used to market the game.

One other category of item that should be included in the full closing kit is the specific tools and middleware that are needed to open any of the archived files. Though most of the programs used during development will be a product in ongoing use (like Autodesk's Maya), a specific version of the software may be required to access a specific file, so you should include that software in the closing kit.

The importance of creating a detailed and accurate closing kit cannot be overstated. The only way an accurate revisiting of the game can take place is if the kit is as thorough as possible. It is helpful to this process if detailed files are kept during the production process for art and sound assets, documents, and build notes. These will assist you later on if you must open the kit for another project, or if you must build patches/fixes for your game.

Interview: Ron Burke, Director/Founder of GamingTrend

Newman: What was your original intention when you created the site GamingTrend.com?

Burke: Well, as you know, we were ConsoleGold prior to rebranding as GamingTrend. All of the political hoopla aside, I was looking at the industry as a whole and realizing that the focus on release dates was becoming less and less important. A "Gold" date (the date that a game is certified as ready for mass production and release) was far less important than the final product. We also wanted to expand our coverage to fill the void that is, to this day, getting larger on PC coverage. Not many know this but I am a PC gamer at heart—I can't let that coverage die just because the industry is heavily focused on the console side of things.

Newman: Over the years, what major changes or trends in game development have impressed you the most or at least created a major impression on you?

Burke: As I just mentioned, there is clearly a large movement towards the console market. Obviously developing for console platforms that don't change in terms of graphics, sound, and other various and sundry components is a lot easier than coding for every graphics card under the sun. Less obvious I think is the gaming press movement towards less detail-oriented reviews.

The focus has shifted towards "funny" reviews that don't necessarily do the game justice, instead eschewing detail in favor of dragging the game through the mud in some half-hearted attempt at personal celebrity. Although I try to bring a certain level of levity to my writing, this trend is the exact opposite of what we do here at GamingTrend.

Newman: When developers are creating a new title, what elements do you think affect the production the most or deserve extra attention for the game to become a major success?

Burke: Wow—if I knew the answer to this question, companies would snap me up in a heartbeat! For me, the key to success is overall polish. So many games come together at the very last second (the developers behind *Assassin's Creed* described the game as fairly broken until weeks before shipping) but pressure to hit certain dates (Halloween for *Hellgate: London*, for instance) means that the game may ship now only to rely on patches to bring it up to speed. I can't readily name a game that moved from being broken to AAA with a patch. The industry needs to disconnect a bit from the Q4 ship dates and realize that people have more time to play games during the summer. The other element that I find to be crucial is finding a need and filling it. It is the most basic of business premises and it is the one most ignored. THQ saw that we didn't have a hacky-slashy loot-whore fest title to play and released the very successful *Titan Quest*. I wouldn't call that title groundbreaking or original, but they sure found a need and filled it, didn't they?

Newman: Today, the concept of games being "cinematic" is a hot topic. In your opinion, what are some of the things you notice immediately about games that are cinematic or epic in nature?

Burke: You say "cinematic" and "epic" and I immediately think of games like *Mass Effect*. The games that pull it off well don't tell a story as much as allow you to experience the story. Nobody wants to have a "book on tape" experience in place of a story, so the proper mix of narration and the ability to impact the storyline are vital to the completion of a true experience. Let's also realize that "epic" doesn't necessarily mean overly long. Many games try to expand the experience by making players backtrack through retread areas or complete quests that are unnecessarily split into subplots—anyone remember the Triforce collection bits in *The Legend of Zelda: The Wind Walker*? This is unnecessary and often leads to stumbling blocks that prevent players from completing the game. Did you know that fewer than half of the games purchased by gamers are actually completed?

Newman: One of the intended results for creating a cinematic game is to, of course, have the title be picked up for possible film option. Have games been successfully translated to the big screen in the past? What titles do you think have done the best with this?

Burke: The first thing you have to do is define success. *Blood Rayne* cost $22 million to make and made a paltry $2.4 million worldwide—obviously, that is the opposite of success. Similarly, *Wing Commander* cost $30 million to produce and made only $11.5 million in worldwide returns. On the other hand, *Mortal Kombat* cost $20 million to make and skyrocketed to a worldwide gross of $122 million in combined DVD and ticket sales. Obviously, if we are talking simple dollars and cents, *Mortal Kombat* takes the crown. Even the sequel, at $30 million to produce, still managed to squeak out a $52 million return. Success in terms of dollars and success as to whether the movie is any good are obviously two very different things. It also demonstrates that simply spending more money isn't the key to success. I don't think game to movie translations have problems being cinematic, I think they just have the curse of being very poorly written. I can't think of anyone who would have minded if *Wing Commander* followed any of the storylines in any of the games and simply starred the very people featured in those FMV [full-motion video] sequences. Matthew Lillard is simply not Maniac.

Newman: It seems that when the crossover goes the other direction (movies that are either simultaneously or later developed into games), the results have been less than spectacular. Why do you think this is the case?

Burke: There is one sharp edge to the movie to game translation: time. The movie is not often feature-complete until it is very close to release, so developers often spend a year or less creating the games. When you throw into the mix how details both minor and major can change at the discretion of the writing team or the director and you have a recipe for a very fluid design chart. Imagine if Optimus Prime were killed at the end of the recent *Transformers: The Movie* from Michael Bay—obviously the bonus stages that occur in the game after the storyline has ended would have to be rewritten. I can't think of a more difficult schedule to work with than when somebody else holds all of the strings. If the game isn't ready, you have to release it anyway—features will be cut and testing will suffer, as they won't be delaying the movie to be timed with the game. Short development time and a design document that is always in flux is simply a recipe for disaster.

Newman: Having observed the numerous discussions taking place in the many forums on your Web site, what do you think are the major buzz topics in the game industry right now? Is this being reflected in the game development world?

Burke: The buzz word is "censorship". Watching FOX the other day I saw one of their game "experts" claim that *Mass Effect* is a sex simulator that allows users to choose your breast size, sleep with as many people as you want, watch and control full-nudity sexual scenarios, and treat women as disposable sexual objects. Anyone who has played the game can attest that absolutely none of those claims are in any way true, but the word is already out. Uninformed masses will spread that misinformation for miles without checking a single fact, going so far as to write their talking-head political figures of choice to see action against companies like Bioware. In the old days we'd call that slander—today we call it "fair and balanced". As it stands, this sort of nonsense coupled with a broken rating system makes developers less inclined to take any level of risk with more mature content. Violence is okay, but not too much. How much is too much? The ESRB will tell you after your product is finished. Granted, they don't have any sort of specific or measurable content, but you'll just have to trust that this self-hired governing body knows what they're doing despite the fact that there isn't a gamer among them—they know smut! Sex is okay, as long as it is implied and nobody sees a bare ass. Granted, you can see far more sexuality and nudity in any given episode of any late-night TV show, but once again we have to trust the ESRB. Our politicians smell blood in the water and latch onto the buzzword-bingo nonsense of calling out M-rated games fueled by misinformed "experts" with their own axe-grinding agenda at hand. I'm not calling for government control, but I would like to see a greater commitment to making sure that the age ratings are more enforced. This means that the lady in front of me who purchased *Grand Theft Auto: San Andreas* for her pre-teen kid should probably pay a bit more attention.

Newman: When you attend major gaming conventions like E3 and GDC, what are you looking for in a new game title? In what ways have games successfully created a presence at a conference that made you take notice?

Burke: Shows like E3 and GDC are simply "the story so far". I saw a fantastic hour-long look at *Fallout 3* and I wrote up an article that describes what I saw while trying to keep as much personal bias out of it as possible. For me, the key is to just remain as neutral as possible. Unlike some sites, I don't judge the title like I would in a full review until I can play it for myself from beginning to end. I'm also not going to give a product a thumbs-up based on a pre-scripted tech demonstration. If you think that those presentations aren't rehearsed and tweaked to the high heavens, you are sorely mistaken. Any new title that I see at an event needs to have a few elements to catch my eye: a hook and a tendency towards overall polish. Granted, many games come together at the very end of the development cycle, but I shouldn't see a subteen frame rate in a game that is due to be released in a month. The hook is equally important—try to compare the last three Tony Hawk titles and you'll see what I mean. The hook in *Project 8* was the Nail the Trick mode, but it was leveraged as a feature instead. When we got to Proving Ground we saw a greatly expanded "Nail the…" mode, but once again, it was just an expanded feature. When you boil the game down, it is simply you skating around a static world. Maybe it is hard to jazz up a skating title, but there is no excuse for the glut of World War II FPS titles. Come up with a new way to tell the story, tell a different side, or try another war—where are the Vietnam games? The last few budget titles didn't score high enough to count. Rather than answer what makes me take notice at a conference, let's talk about what doesn't make a good impression. Two E3s ago, I was bumped from a floor-level console so an EB Product Manager could take a crack at it. Watching this suit fumble about for a few minutes was painful, and I'm sure he didn't really care about the product, but only how much he was getting paid per square foot of display space. Another thing that doesn't sit well with me is blaring noise. At one particular booth there were not one but two full-size rock bands hammering as hard as they could on their instruments trying to outgun each other. It was loud enough for me to hear through several sound-resistant rooms. As a member of the press, I want to hear about the hook, what is new, what inspired the title, and other various details that fans will be interested to know. Before any of that can happen though, I have to be able to hear.

Newman: What advice would you give a young developer who's trying to create a successful franchise game?

Burke: Creating a franchise game is a pretty difficult proposition. Kaz Hirai once said that the consumer doesn't really know what they want. At the time I was pretty offended by this statement, but time has proven him wise. Most consumers sit back and wait for the new concepts to come to them. I think that companies like Bioware and Square Enix have it right—they don't worry as much about the mechanics as they do about telling an interesting and engaging story. *Kane and Lynch* may have had an interesting story tucked away in there, but I couldn't care less about the characters. You can't be immersed in something you don't care about. Similarly, make sure your story makes sense—I'm talking to you Kojima-san! I'm not sure what turning into a statue and grabbing the genitals of a nearby statue, or eyeballing scantily clad women in a magazine has to do with saving the world from mooing/hopping Metal Gear robots, but I am already pretty perplexed by *Metal Gear Solid 4: Sons of the Patriots*. If you want to see how it is done, take a look at *Uncharted: Drake's Fortune*—the game features a likeable and realistic person in a semi-plausible adventure story that takes place in a believable framework. More than anything, be willing to take a few risks. Without risk, we would never have seen such fantastic titles as the *Sam & Max* series, *Psychonauts*, and *Spore*.

Part 2

INCORPORATING CINEMATIC SKILLS

Now that we have taken a look at the current development model, we will cover the film industry processes and practices that can be applied to game development to create a more epic and cinematic title. Some of the areas that will be covered in Part 2 include writing, character development, storyboarding, cinematography, directing, and casting.

One of the most fundamental beliefs in the film industry is that a movie is only as good as the original screenplay. Without a script that is anything less than brilliant, your chances at producing a successful film are slim. Often, the development period of a film is solely about getting the final version of the script in place. This could mean bringing in many different writers, creating many different drafts of the script, and numerous meetings involving the taking of notes and making improvements on the story. Taking a vested interest in a game's story and characters is the first step in creating a cinematic title.

5

WRITER

Of all the jobs within the game industry, that of the writer is probably the least defined and most misunderstood. Sometimes an actual writer is hired to script the game, but more often than not the script is formulated by the creative director or the producers involved with the game. This runaround becomes evident in some titles through the sheer lack of good story and an overabundance of paper-thin characters contained within the game. In the past, I've dealt with producers who regard the role of the writer as writing the dialogue spoken by the characters in-game. This approach is indicative of the ignorance concerning what a writer actually does and the lack of concern the game industry has for story.

While writing this book, the Writer's Guild of America was involved in a strike and petitioning for better compensation. Believe me, the effects of this are being felt in Hollywood and throughout the television and film industries! This is mostly because these industries are clearly aware of the importance regarding good writing. Nothing is as important to the success of a film as the script. This approach needs to be used more often in game development. Imagine the impact that a great story will have on a gamer when coupled with the interactivity of awesome game play.

Clearly, some titles have made more of an effort than others to set a higher bar regarding story and characters—games like the popular *Halo* series, the Tom Clancy branded titles and even horror-based games (like *Silent Hill* and *Resident Evil*) have decidedly better production value in this regard. Coincidentally, *Silent Hill* and *Resident Evil* have both already been produced as movies, while *Tom Clancy's Splinter Cell* and *Halo* are currently being developed for the big screen as well.

Another bad practice in the game industry regarding writing is not starting to write a script until well into the production cycle.

The writing in Capcom's *Resident Evil* series contributes to the overall atmosphere and horror of the game. Reproduced by permission of Capcom U.S.A., Inc. All rights reserved.

This error is completely unacceptable if you want an immersive, cinematic game. The script should most definitely be honed in preproduction or during the concept phase and turned in as soon as possible to allow the game designers and all concerned to have some sort of map regarding the story before production begins. It's true that some game studios have been burned in the past by writers (usually because the writer placed the need for a great story above the costs of changing the game's design), but it is still a good idea to have the writer in place during preproduction, if for no other reason than to help create a sort of flowchart or formal outline for the story.

The first step in recognizing and fostering good writing in the game community is to standardize some of the writing processes involved with game development. There are several cinematic cues that can be taken from the film community concerning this.

5.1   Format and Script Development

Unlike the game industry, the film industry has had a standard script format for quite some time. The benefit of this is obvious: writers know exactly how to write for a project and what is expected from them when turning a script in. Even the processes for *developing* a great script have been honed to empower the screen writer with the tools necessary for completion. Though many writers may disagree on what exactly constitutes good content for a script and what different literary tools and images should be used within the pages, all screen writers can agree on what the final script should look and read like.

As mentioned earlier, the game industry has many different ways for writing game scripts. Most of the problems involved with writing has centered around the difficulty of dealing with all the possibilities of interactivity. A screenplay may have only one path concerning what will happen in a movie or television program, but a game may have multiple paths. For a game to be as enjoyable as possible there *should* be many paths that a gamer can choose to take. Each of these paths must be scripted and accounted for. How does a writer do this?

The *Lord of the Rings Online* series of games from Turbine features many paths that a gamer can take. The artwork appearing to the left is copyright protected and reproduced with permission. © 2008 Turbine, Inc. All rights reserved. This publication is in no way endorsed or sponsored by Turbine, Inc. or its licensors.

There are several popular methodologies regarding multiple-path writing, but the two most popular seem to be the "multiple columns" approach and the "choose your path" book approach. Either way, for complete coverage of the game, game writing should center around the use of events, decisions, or locales—and should contain some methodology for tagging dialogue to these.

The use of multiple columns is already prevalent in screenplays; in fact, most screenplay programs that are in use have this function already included (sometimes this is referred to as a "dual dialogue" function). In this game writing methodology, you write the action, present a choice, and then approach the different choices available to the gamer in a separate column beneath the action. If, after the decisions of the gamer have been made, the end result is singular and the next scene or piece of action will be the same regardless of choice, this is probably the best method for writing the script. However, if there are truly many different ways to play and finish the game (meaning some paths are never explored during game play), consider the technique of using a "choose your path" book style of writing.

"Choose your own path" books have been around forever; essentially, you read a portion of the book, a choice is given, you make a decision regarding what you want to do, and then you turn to the appropriate page to pick up the action based upon your decision. When employing this method for writing your game script, the various pieces of action are written, then connected using hyperlinks and bookmarks. Though this type of writing does not resemble a screenplay, in some circumstances, it can better serve a project. Because most games do have a definite ending and game levels are limited, it is usually the intent of most developers to make the entire game playable in every session. That said, there's no reason why most games cannot be made using a standard screenplay format. But don't let the format for the script hang you up!

Having read for several major screen writing competitions (the Austin Film Festival's, for one), I have seen many great stories passed over due to poor formatting and style. As a gaming writer, you will not have to face such harsh scrutiny! Instead, you can use the best practices of script development to help write a great story for your game using the best format possible.

Though it may be difficult to actually sum up what makes a story great, there are several main components of a great story that can identified. The first is the use of well-developed characters. The creation of a memorable protagonist and antagonist is the first step towards writing an epic story.

Development Tip

Download a copy of the free software Celtx today (http://www.celtx.com). It's a script formatting program that also has features that help develop your story and characters, as well as track changes made to the script.

5.2   Character Development

The protagonist, to put it simply, is the hero of the story—and within a game, is also the gamer! Creating a great main character is the cornerstone of the script. Great examples of this already exist in the game world—who doesn't know Master Chief of *Halo* fame, or Sam Fisher, the undercover agent in *Tom Clancy's Splinter Cell*? Not only will your protagonist fulfill a great need of the gamer, but he/she can supply your game with a calling-card franchise character. There are several characteristics that mark a great protagonist.

Ubisoft's *Tom Clancy's Splinter Cell* series is anchored by the great character Sam Fisher. Reproduced by permission of UbiSoft. All rights reserved.

Film guru Robert McKee states, "A protagonist is a willful character," in his seminal book *Story*. It is in the examination of the character's "willfulness" that will create the motivation for your main character, as well as define a past that is relevant to the present within the game. Sometimes this is called a "back story". Although a back story can be extremely useful for answering some of the why's involved with the game, it should be used only in a way that provides motivation for the character in the story. Writing a lengthy back story only bogs down the game and story and detracts from the game play.

In addition to brainstorming the particulars of your characters (background, ethnicity, profession, and so on), the main *goal* of the protagonist should also be defined. It is the goal of the protagonist that forms the plot of the game. Though there are many different ways to approach creating just such a character, perhaps one of the best ways of defining your protagonist is to create a pertinent antagonist.

The antagonist is usually the "bad guy" in the game. When created correctly, the antagonist actually complements the protagonist. Maybe they are rivals with much in common. Maybe they completely contrast against each other in both personality and substance. A great way to craft a memorable antagonist is to give him or her an opposing goal; this can be as simple as the antagonist's goal being to stop the protagonist's goal (or vice versa) or it can be the same goal, putting the two characters in direct competition. Either way, having a great villain is another useful way to add production value to your script. Games that have a memorable antagonist go a long way towards being cinematic.

Once you have created the main characters, it's time to move on to the major supporting characters. It's a good idea when creating the sidebar characters to include various demographics not covered by the two main characters. Want female gamers to buy your game? Have a great female character. Not only does this help with broadening your audience, but it adds variation and diversity to your story. Use character breakdown sheets when developing the various details involved with creating the characters (see the sample character breakdown sheet in Appendix A: Extras).

When you are developing characters, keep in mind that the interactive aspects of gaming should be coming into play! One of the more fun ways to develop an interactive story is to allow for changes in a character's personality versus changes in the environment. In other words, instead of having a player choose between taking the rickety bridge across the river or swimming for it, have the player choose between killing innocent soldiers on the bridge to get across or risking his or her own life swimming across dangerous waters. As a game progresses, a character can become more "evil" or "good" based upon decisions the gamer has made and this can change the options made available to the gamer.

When all the major characters have been defined and created, you can now move on to identifying the major theme(s) contained within the game.

5.3 Themes and Symbolism

Think of the theme as the lesson to be learned from the story. It doesn't have to be preachy. It can be as simple as "crime doesn't pay" or "you can't escape fate". Whatever the theme is, it can usually be summed up by the original intent of the game creator. What was the original message you wanted to project to the world when you formed the original concept of the game? Perhaps the game was conceived to fulfill a particular vacuum in the gaming industry. What was this? This overall idea should be considered as an outline before the script is developed and the particulars of the story are discussed. It is an important task for the writer to keep the script within the theme of the story.

Some argue that a theme is unnecessary in a game and that a game should be squarely created around fun and features. This is fine. Even if there is no grand underlying idea in the game, working with basic emotions, motivations, and desires of the characters strengthens the story contained within the game.

The game *Assassin's Creed* from Ubisoft is full of topical themes regarding the Middle East, religion, and cultural differences. Reproduced by permission of UbiSoft. All rights reserved.

One of the tools that the writer often uses to keep the story within the original theme is the use of cleverly placed symbols. This is called "symbolism". Symbolism can be an extremely complicated affair or as simple as the use of a prop. An example of prop symbolism could be a wedding ring that represents the love of the protagonist for his wife and family or a lucky keepsake that goes missing (and when it's found, the luck of the character returns with it).

Symbolism can also be a very complicated thing such as placing enough references to an evil organization or corporation to make the gamer think of a particular religion or government. Either way, the use of strategic symbols and symbolic props is another method for getting production value into the script and game. When coupled with the best practices involved with constructing a solid script, a great story is created. The use of symbolism, though, should be supported by the theme of the story and not just placed within the game in an attempt to make the game "deep".

The use of the many best practices of screenwriters will help you develop your script. These best practices can be summed up with three major elements: story, plot, and scenes. When used together, these three elements add up to give your script a well-defined structure.

5.4 Structure

A great structure means getting your protagonist from Point A (the beginning of the game) to Point B (the end) in the most entertaining way possible. Although this is determined to a great extent by the *goal* of the main character, actions are also influenced by the various outside elements involved within the story. To begin the process of creating good structure, the story must first be broken down into a basic group of manageable chunks (scenes) that move the story forward in the desired direction.

The script should be able to be broken down into scenes relatively easily. In the film industry, this is called "breaking down" a script. When you have broken down the script, you should be able to easily identify the individual levels and areas of play within the game. Sometimes, it will also identify key sections in the script that will not be able to be included in the game play. In a game, this usually means that a connecting cut-scene will have to be created.

Scenes are the smallest unit of measurement in a script—usually just a few minutes—and have a beginning, middle, and end. In a game, this can be introducing a new level, a new location, or sudden shift in action. A new scene can also be created when a new character is introduced. Once you have mapped all the scenes/levels out, place each of the scenes under a magnifying glass. Ask these questions: Is the scene important? What are the goals that are trying to be accomplished? Would this scene stand up on its own?

Every scene needs to be exciting and fresh to the gamer. If a scene does not have what it takes, take a look at the elements involved and decide what needs to be changed.

Perhaps changing the location (keeping in mind that this could be creating another level that will need to be created within the game) or a twist in the story that's unexpected (one of your squad members turns on you!) would make the scene better. Whichever method you use, make sure that it is consistent with the overall feel and style of the game and within the original concept! There can be multiple writers involved with a game, so it will become a huge task to ensure that they all adhere to this. Once the scenes have all been honed and are the best they can each be individually, you should be able to see a coherent story contained within the script. If the story is not coherent, it will become evident fast when the quality assurance team starts to dissect the game during production.

The final element involved with defining good structure is that of plot. If you're thinking of what constitutes the story as "this is what happens", you can think of the plot as "this is *why* it happens". Basically, it's cause and effect—motivation and reasons on the part of the characters. Setting up a good reason for the protagonist to take on the mob makes the game more believable. Is it revenge? Is it the desire to rule the underworld? Both are great plots and both contribute to creating completely different scripts. Once the story, plot, and individual scenes have been articulated, you can approach writing the actual first draft of the script.

Most Hollywood movies are actually written in what is called a "three-act structure". The famous screenwriter Syd Field first wrote about this method of writing a script many years ago in his book *Screenplay*. Basically, the three act approach consists of dividing a script into three major sections: the setup, the confrontation, and the resolution.

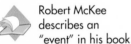

Development Tip

Robert McKee describes an "event" in his book *Story* as something that creates change. This is a good rule of thumb. When events happen in the game, they should have meaning. The more meaningful each event is that occurs, the deeper the immersion the gamer will experience, and the more cinematic the production.

5.5   Three-Act Structure

Many screen writers today do their best to avoid using the typical three-act structure (many feel the approach is clichéd), but almost all finished scripts end up presenting a story in this fashion. Though it is sometimes considred to be predictable, the truth of the matter is that there is nothing more basic to a story than having a beginning, middle, and end. Avoiding an ending doesn't just "buck the system". It creates an undesirable aftermath when the game is over and leaves behind an unsatisfied gamer. You don't want to leave your audience hanging…unless of course, you are planning a sequel that will be picking the story up again!

The first act of the screenplay, also known as the setup, is about getting the protagonist in motion. This means creating an "inciting incident". The inciting incident is the event that occurs that gets the protagonist on the path to resolution. Examples of a setup include the moment in *Elder Scrolls IV: Oblivion*, when the king is killed and the gamer is set on the quest to restore the throne and the opening level in *Call of Duty 4: Modern Warfare*, where an assassination prompts the United States and the United Kingdom to scramble special operations troops to prevent a world incident. Whatever your inciting incident is, it must be compelling and warrant the gamer investing time in playing the game.

The beginning of the script should also focus on setting up the situation that your protagonist is getting into and the basic locations that will be visited. This focus lays down the foundation for the tone of the game; is this about adventure and exotic locations, or is the tone more subdued and familiar? Once the foundations of the story have been laid in the first act, you can then move on to the second act.

Activision's *Call of Duty 4: Modern Warfare* uses a strong story structure to carry the game's narrative. Reproduced by permission of Activision. All rights reserved.

Act II of a three-act script is also called the confrontation. Another way of looking at the second act is to think of it as creating conflict. It's an old Hollywood axiom that most scripts fall apart in the second act. The writer created a great character, set up a great opening scene and inciting incident, then failed to move the story forward in any way. The second act of your script should be about conflict. What is standing in the protagonist's way? This can be handled by focusing on the antagonist or by creating obstacles that now stand in the way of the protagonist. The best screenplays exploit both paths. In the gaming world, though, it is best to concentrate on creating obstacles. By doing so, the gamer is presented with a series of

Development Tip

If you are having difficulty getting a specific level honed to perfection. Think of the scene as a series of beats. A "beat" is a specific action that moves the plot forward within the scene. By breaking down a level by each action, you can create an accurate mini-map of what happens in a specific level.

challenges that must be overcome within levels. This presents many opportunities for awarding the gamer with achievements and increasing the level of immersion in the game.

Once the meat of your script has been created in the second act, you can then move on to the third and final act. The final section of the script should be centered around the concept of resolution. The final levels of the game should test the player's resolve to finish the game, as well as create moments that resolve the various elements of the story. A great story provides the gamer with some level of resolution. Once again, think of the central theme of the story. A great resolution not only brings the game to a satisfactory ending (usually by allowing the protagonist to "win"), but also supports the central theme of the story: good conquers evil, or there is no fate, or even order suppresses individuality.

That said, once you have broken down the basic three acts of your script, you can now divide each act into a group of smaller, individual scenes or levels that you have crafted. Each of these scenes move each act towards the inevitable ending of the game. At this point, the major conflicts involved with the story, and the resolution, should be blatantly obvious. Make sure you include the necessary scenes that will bring your story to completion; necessary scenes (also called master scenes) are those that directly support the resolution of the story. You will also want to have scenes that concentrate on the game's subplots (especially if there is a love story or back story that can be visited through the use of flashbacks). The three-act structure can assist you in completing the first draft (and subsequent drafts) of the game script.

Check out *Far Cry Instincts: Predator* by Ubisoft to see a game with a great three-act story. Reproduced by permission of UbiSoft. All rights reserved.

Again, as there are no standards in formatting, it is perfectly acceptable to approach writing your game script like writing a movie script—it can even help you later on (if the game garners attention for possible optioning, you will already have a recognizable script that can be circulated as part of a movie pitch). As the drafts of the script get closer and closer to where you want it, you will begin to see a certain style emerge that is reflective of the script writer(s). Pay attention to this style. When rewrites occur later on in production because a level was suddenly cut, you will want to have the writer available who contributed to this in the biggest way.

5.6 Style

Creating a great script, even in the best of circumstances, is usually a collaborative effort. Though one person may be credited as the original writer of the script or the creator of the story, chances are good that many different people had creative input into the final version of a script. This is good—many brains are better than a single brain. When a creative director is great at communicating his or her vision, it becomes a much easier task to work in a uniform style. But at some point, you will identify a person (or persons) that will become the responsible writer for the finished product. This will probably be because of the *style* of that writer.

Though style is a tough thing to define, it's best thought of as the synergy involved with creating dialogue and action that is indicative of the original vision and concept of the game—it also points to characteristics that make up an individual's technique. Once you identify individuals who are in sync with this (and hopefully make them integral to the creative team), let them do their jobs. When given the tools necessary for them to understand the overall concept of the game, they will craft the final draft of the script you need for developing a successful title.

The collaboration involved with putting the story all together with a satisfying ending can be an awesome experience. Just remember when writing your script to keep the action moving, the dialogue fresh and memorable, and add enough twists and conflict to keep the gamer guessing; remember, the protagonist doesn't have to win all the time!

Interview: Daniel Erickson, Writer at BioWare

Daniel Erickson started his career at Imagine Media (now Future) as an intern at *Next Generation* magazine. From there, he helped launch DailyRadar.com and wrote for several other publications, including PC Game and Games Business. He jumped the fence into development by going to work at EA Canada, working

Development Tip

When creating a unique style within a script, there are several different literary devices at your disposal. These include the use of a false ending (also known as the "fakeout"), subplots that become the main plot, and the killing of main characters. All of these are referred to as the story making a "right turn". Including right turns in your script will keep the story interesting and free of cliché.

Daniel Erickson

on the first three *NBA Street* titles, first as a producer and eventually doing lead design work on *NBA Street* Vol. 2 and 3.

In 2005, Daniel chased his long-time dream and went to work for BioWare to work on *Dragon Age*, the RPG company's upcoming epic fantasy game. From there, he moved down to the newly formed Austin studio and is currently Principal Lead Writer there for the studio's first title, an as-of-yet unannounced MMO project.

Newman: Explain briefly your background in the gaming industry.
Erickson: I started as a critic for the now-defunct *Next Generation* magazine and did some freelance work for several other magazines as well. I then jumped the fence to game design, cutting my teeth at EA Canada working on the EA Sports BIG franchises (*NBA Street, SSX*). Once I had a couple of titles under my belt as lead designer, I made my way to BioWare, which had always been my dream, and took a job as a full-time writer.

Newman: How long have you been specifically involved with game writing?
Erickson: Three years working on just writing, but I did all of the writing on the games that I was doing design work on before as well. So seven years overall.

Newman: In your experience, do you feel that the vocation of game writing has been hurt or helped by the lack of a standard format (such as the script standard used in the film industry)?
Erickson: Neither, really. Different formats are developed for different types of games. Books don't use the same format as magazines for layout and those two are more similar to each other than the writing on *Madden* is to the writing on *Mass Effect*. It's not the difference in subject matter; it's the difference in what that writing is used for. In *Madden*, it's small pieces written for particular situations that are then stitched together on the fly, and so need to live in databases. Excel really is the easiest for handling that. *Mass Effect*, in stark contrast, is mainly a series of interactive, branching conversations that can only be written in a custom tool built specifically for such things.

Newman: When constructing a new script for a game, what specific elements do you look for to improve the overall gaming experience?
Erickson: Pacing, pacing, pacing. The balance between dialogue and action, the timing of rewards, the dissemination of knowledge and plot at a pace the player can respond to and absorb. Game writing is at least half game design.

Newman: How do you develop these beyond the initial script?
Erickson: Constant review and play testing. Design *is* testing and iteration. Writing *is* rewriting.

Newman: In the film industry, it's common practice for writers to construct detailed backgrounds and back stories to each character in the movie. Is this necessary in the game industry?

Erickson: Depends on the game. We have literally thousands of pages of background details on the project I'm working on now, and most RPGs have at least a solid background story for each character and event. Even when working on *NBA Street Vol. 2*, I still found it extremely helpful for both myself and the artists to have dossiers on each of the characters. I'm not sure it's absolutely necessary in a run-and-gun shooter, but it can only help.

Newman: How does a story benefit from having a more fleshed-out cast?

Erickson: You simply can't write believable lines for a character you don't know. You must have that voice in your head and be able to have your little schizophrenic conversations with it. Without that, you have just hollow characters mouthing the plot.

Newman: Typically, does a game script contain the same three-act structure of a film? How do you outline the story within a game title?

Erickson: This varies hugely. The three-act structure is a good place to start, but if you're writing a twenty-hour game you may have more than three acts, or you may, more likely, have several three-act arcs—more like a movie series or a TV show season. Outlining, of course, varies widely. On an RPG, you're dealing with such a huge beast that the outline itself can be hundreds of pages and take months of work. For a racing game, a couple pages might do it.

Newman: As a video game is interactive (and a film is not), what particular challenges rise when scripting possible pathways for a player?

Erickson: The magic and the frustration of interactive fiction (not games punctuated by cut scenes) is that you must remove the essential tool of traditional writing: the protagonist. The payoff is the trade for player agency, which is everything appealing about fiction in this format, but it's a jump many writers are unable to make. People will continually wonder how you would make *Citizen Kane* as a game if you can't force the character to say "Rosebud". Well, of course, you can't. You also can't make *Citizen Kane* into a ballet. They are different storytelling mediums and the sooner game writers wake up to that and get over their inferiority complexes, the sooner they'll be able to start creating great works in their own medium.

Newman: If a game student wanted to embark upon a career of writing for games, where would you direct him or her?

Erickson: The great thing about games right now is that it's still sort of the Wild West out here. Less so than fifteen years ago, clearly, but a kid with great talent and dedication can still get their foot in the door somewhere. BioWare, for instance, has a couple of fantastic writers that came straight out of school. If you're talented, I'm not in the slightest interested in your resume. While you're waiting for that break, though, play as many of the type of games you want to write as you can get your hands on and really analyze what makes them work and what you would improve. Then find something easily mod-able (*Neverwinter Nights* is great for this and takes no tech knowledge) and practice, practice, practice. Additionally, some of the game design schools are starting to teach game writing, but that's still fairly rare.

Newman: Do you think this field will continue to grow within the game industry as a standalone job or do you think writing will be viewed as a function of the game designer or creative director?

Erickson: For any company that cares about great writing, this will always be a standalone job and as VO [Voice Over] budgets balloon into the millions of dollars, it only makes sense to pay for great content to put in the actors' mouths. There is no comparison between a level designer slumming on some dialogue and a gifted writer who's been studying storytelling for ten years.

6

STORYBOARD AND CONCEPT ART

The use of concept art has been widespread in the game industry for some time, though the use of storyboarding is not as common a practice. Storyboarding is basically designing a series of sketches that illustrate how the story will unfold—much like individual panels in a comic book. They can be as simple as a sketch or as complicated as computer-generated graphics with motion. Either way, the purpose of the storyboards is to illustrate how the story will unfold within the parameters of the scene (time, location, and so on) and to help the team to understand the technical aspects of the frame, such as camera location, camera movement, and types of shots that will be used.

Concept art, on the other hand, are static art pieces created in great detail that help the development team understand what individual characters, locations, and scenes will look like. Concept art (and even storyboard art) can be helpful when you are making your initial pitch to a publisher and can get your team working with a unified vision for what the game will look like. They can also help programmers to understand the individual assets that will be involved with developing each level.

Making a detailed set of storyboards for each level will also do things that the basic concept art cannot. Concept art is used to establish the artistic elements of a particular character or location (level) and helps the animators and artists understand what those elements are supposed to look like. This includes the color scheme, lighting, and style of the art. Think of the storyboards as the tech side of the illustrations. The storyboards will illustrate how the character is supposed to get from Point A to Point B within the level/scene, what props will be present in the level, and the way the scene will actually look from a technical

An example of concept art from Capcom's *Lost Planet.* Reproduced by permission of Capcom U.S.A., Inc. All rights reserved.

aspect: Where is the camera located? Is a cut-scene needed? What will the gamer see when moving across the level?

Another great perk to the use of storyboards is the ability to experiment without the investment of much money. Taking the time to illustrate various ways to tell the story (flashbacks, playing with the timeline, and so on) can help determine which approach will create and evoke the most emotional payoff, as well as create the highest possible level of suspense or drama within the game.

6.1   Using Basic Design Documentation

As the basic design document will already contain a lot of information regarding the game, it can be used to help your artists create the storyboards needed for each level. The key things that should be extracted from the document include the story, the game features that will be used within the game (and set it apart from preceding games), and the major characters within the game. Getting the look of the major locations and characters down early on is a no-brainer, but how about the major features? For instance, if one of the game features includes the ability for the gamer to jump across great distances in the blink of an eye, this is something that can be illustrated in a series of storyboards. Not only will it give a visual representation of the feature, but it will give you a means for showing the publisher and team how that feature will actually work within the confines of the game.

Once the storyboards are actually finished, they can actually complement the design documentation and be an additional tool for the producers, engineers, and animators to use when hammering out production. They will also help you in a very basic manner: the more the game is actually storyboarded, the more focused the team will be on the actual levels that are being designed. This means that the budget will not be affected as heavily by reworking levels to accommodate new props and assets, as those would have been previsualized during the storyboarding process.

6.2   Seeing the Story

Being aware of the individual elements of each level/scene is very important. Putting them on paper before the programmers invest hundreds of hours of work into creating a level is a great way to keep from impacting your budget in a negative way. If you are creating a game that will feature cut-scenes within it, the storyboards will also provide a means to actually seeing how the game will transition between the levels and the cut-scenes and how the scenes can be kept pertinent to the gamer. Taking the time to will also illustrates any major holes in the story; because a series of storyboards is quite similar to that of a comic strip or graphic novel, the viewer should be able to look at the storyboards and *see* the story. If the team cannot determine the story from the visual cues within the storyboards, then there's probably work that still needs to be done from the storytelling aspect.

Never underestimate the visual impact of games like those in the *Resident Evil* series. Reproduced by permission of Capcom U.S.A., Inc. All rights reserved.

Development Tip

Because most storyboards are made during the preproduction process, you may not have actual artists/ animators working with the team at this point—and if you do, they are probably more focused on getting the concept art together. Consider using a computer storyboards program like FrameForge 3D Studio to do the work. In addition to helping with placement (you can move props around independently within the program), a program can actually show camera movement and character movement within the scene/level.

Another key way that storyboards are used in the film industry is to help determine locations. As the locations are so vital to the look and appeal of a film and game, it is important that each level is impacted by *where* it takes place. It is not uncommon for producers to have no idea where a scene should take place (at least specific locations—it may be determined early on to feature combat on a skyscraper, but *which* skyscraper? What kind of skyscraper?), but once it is actually drawn in the form of a storyboard, location ideas will come to light.

6.3   Nonlinear Thinking

A video game is made up of quite a few independent levels, characters, and scenes; it is better to think of the individual components as complementary assets rather than thinking of the game in a timeline like Level 1, Level 2, and so on. Divide the story into the separate elements, including the character profiles, locations, events that will take place, history of the situations, and related story issues. Once you have the concept art pieces for the characters and locations completed, you can then move on to the designing of the actual scenes.

When you begin sketching out the main levels as they would appear to the gamer, the storyboards can point out major holes in the game play, as well as allow the game designer to determine the types and quantity of props within the level. This will be helpful when planning exactly what the gamer will be able to interact with and what will be static scenery within the game.

A great way to tackle the storyboarding of a level is to use a method known as "reverse storyboarding". As the designers probably know how the level is supposed to end for the gamer, storyboard that scene first. Then work your way back through the individual scenes and levels towards the opening picture. Again, because this is working the level in a nonlinear way, it will help keep the individual steps in the level independent and give each of them their own strengths. Most game levels are in many ways self-contained, so working them out of order should present few problems. You can also use screenshots to set up a flowchart that illustrates the various paths that a game can take and how they relate to each other—which is very useful, as you want gamers to be able to take different approaches to playing the game.

Some great questions to ask as you are storyboard a level are: What type of camera placement is ideal for this scene? Are there any important props or vehicles in the level? What environment elements will affect the scene—is it day or night? Rainy or fair weather? Does all the action take place inside, outside, or both? Is any special lighting necessary? What kinds of special effects will take place—explosions? Fires? These are all questions that can be answered within the storyboards.

Midway's game *Blacksite: Area 51* uses solid framing and camera techniques to maximize the production value of environments within the game. Reproduced by permission of Midway Games. All rights reserved.

6.4   Storyboarding Process

The storyboarding phase consists of four different tasks:

1. *Decide the format and detail of the storyboards.* As the individual illustrations can be made in any size, it's best to determine the screen ratio that the game will be projected in and then use the appropriate ratio in the storyboards. Will the game be a "fit the television" game (usually called 4:3 ratio in the film industry) or will it be in a wide-screen format (or both)? Also, in how much detail will the scene be illustrated? Do you want a storyboard for every action that takes place in the level, or will it be necessary to storyboard only the key moments?

2. *Create thumbnails.* These are basic drawings that are small (the size of a thumbnail if necessary) and contain very little detail. The purpose of the thumbnails is to just get the placement of the individual assets within the level and to show the viewpoint of the scene—that is, what the camera angle will be. In the film industry, many directors get by with creating only thumbnail storyboards. Because concept art generally illustrates the look of the scene, as well as the color schemes and similar details that are involved, the storyboards need show only the staging of the scene. With a video game, it will probably be necessary to move on to the next step.

3. *Create 2D storyboards.* Now that we have the format of the drawings and the thumbnails have been created, we can move on to creating a higher-quality rendition of each level/scene. In addition to doing the same things that the thumbnails do (specifically, the layout and camera angle of each scene), the purpose of the 2D storyboards is to capture the mood or emotion of each scene. Is it a dark moment within the game? Does the lighting capture that? Care must be taken, though, to not create storyboards/images that cannot be captures in the game. At this point, the game designers and producers should be consulting with the storyboard artist to insure that each scene is storyboarded accurately. Once high-quality 2D storyboards are created, the team can move on to the use of 3D storyboards if needed.

4. *Create 3D storyboards.* This step involves the use of a storyboarding program or animation software. Although it's completely acceptable to make 3D storyboards with the use of Maya, 3ds Max, or Lightweave, most storyboard artists prefer to use either a filmmaking storyboard program or to use 3D models from Poser or DAZ Studio. The advantage of using 3D storyboards is that the development team can actually see how the level will look to the gamer, how to use lighting, and to adjust camera angles. Some storyboarding programs even have the ability to have movement in the frame so you can see how a character can move within the scene. Moving storyboards are usually called "animatics" and have been wide used in the animated film industry.

6.5 Cut-Scenes

If it has been determined in preproduction that the game will include cut-scenes, storyboards can be especially helpful in this arena. As cut-scenes mean that the gamer will not be interacting with the action, they can be thought of as mini-movies within the game. In this respect, the storyboard process can be approached exactly like that of a film. In addition to the illustration pane, each drawing can feature a description panel underneath that explains any important information that is not in the storyboard. The description panel can sometimes include information regarding dialogue, special effects, or camera movement—usually, though, the camera movement in indicated in the actual panel with use of arrows.

Zoom In on Action

Example of a storyboard
with camera movement and
description.

As you construct the storyboard sequence for the cut-scene, think of the illustrations as a comic book or graphic novel; the drawings should move forward in a logical narrative and tell the story visually. This can be easily accomplished by making a short "script" that describes for the artist what should appear in each panel that will be created. The basic storyboarding process can be described in the following four-step process:

Step 1: Framing. Once you know the size of the storyboard, you must first determine the size of the objects within the frame. This can usually be done by determining the type of shot that is within the scene. By simply marking the storyboard as a long shot or a medium shot, the artist can then determine the size of the characters, props, and so on within the frame. The different types of shots are discussed in the chapter on cinematography.

Step 2: Camera Angle. Will the viewpoint be from down low, or high above the characters? Note on the storyboard whether the camera will be on an even "eye line" (straight in front of or behind the characters), a high angle, or low angle.

Step 3: Depth of Field. This is the same thing as a cinematographer choosing a lens. How much of the scene will be in focus? Do you want everything to be crystal-clear (like in documentary footage), or will the background be blurred? How far will the background be from the objects in the foreground? The choice of depth of field is an artistic decision and can affect the emotional impact of the scene, so choose carefully.

Step 4: Movement. If there is going to be any movement within the frame, it must be annotated either within the frame with arrows or beneath the frame with a description panel. Either way,

The use of an overhead camera angle helps reinforce how small you within the scope of the universe when you begin playing the game *Spore*. © 2006 Electronic Arts Inc. Electronic Arts, EA, the EA logo and Spore are trademarks or registered trademarks of Electronic Arts Inc. in the U.S. and/or other countries. All rights reserved. All other trademarks are the property of their respective owners. EA™ is an Electronic Arts™ brand.

all movement (including the camera itself) must be indicated for the artist.

Once all these steps have been taken and the storyboards are scripted, the artist can now create a graphic representation of what your cut-scene will look like. This storyboard will be the roadmap that the animators and artists use when creating the scene.

6.6 Storyboards and Interactive Media

In addition to use within the film industry to help with setting up and designing individual shots in a movie, storyboards have also been used recently to help with the designing and maintaining of interactive media and Web sites. As Web sites can also incorporate audio, video, and graphic elements in a nonlinear fashion, storyboards are a great way to illustrate the various ways the site can interact with visitors. In this sense, the storyboards can be looked at as a sort of flowchart or site map that shows the interactivity of the individual elements of the Web page. This can help when designing the online site for the game you are producing.

It is also becoming more prevalent within the game industry to involve an "alternative reality game" (ARG) with the release of a title. Bungie's *Halo 2* was preceded with the ARG "I Love Bees", *Halo 3* was kicked off by the ARG "Iris", and even television series are now using the concept of an ARG (the program *Lost* held an online ARG called the "Lost Experience"). Because alternative reality games usually include online content that is meant to interact with live action performed by the gamer in the real world, storyboards are a great way to map out how events will unfold between the Web site and reality, as well as the path that the gamers will take in the real world while exploring the game.

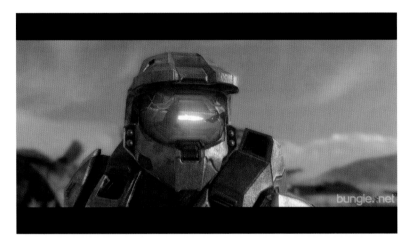

The *Halo 3* alternate reality game help fuel the fire of anticipation before the game's release.

Interview: Mathieu Raynault, Digital Matte Painter

Mathieu Raynault is a digital matte painter (digital matte painting is the art of creating traditional matte paintings—usually background/environment work—electronically, using a combination of scanning, drawing, and coloring using a computer and specially designed software) and has worked on films like *300*, *Star Wars: Episode II Attack of the Clones*, two of the *Lord of the Rings* films, and *King Kong*. In addition to his film experience, he has also produced art for television and the game industries (*Prince of Persia III*, *The Act of War*, and *Men of Valor*). You can see examples of his work on his Web site (http://www.raynault.com).

Newman: Typically, what kind of information is given to you by a client regarding a new scenic piece? Is it usually very detailed information, or do you generally get a lot of room to inject your own artistic input into the scene?

Raynault: It really depends on the project. I do often have to provide sketches and concepts early in the process in order to start dialog with the director or art director. In these cases I am involved early, and my creative input is quite significant. Though, sometime like on *Star Wars* for example, I would get a pretty detailed concept art piece, basically a painting that was done by one of Lucas's concept artist, establishing composition, color palette, mood and lighting. On cases like this, my job becomes solely to create the most believable photorealistic image based on the concept.

Newman: You've produced art for film and game projects. What has been some of the major differences with working in these two industries?

Raynault: It's been quite similar in fact. My contribution to video games was on cinematics only which are basically short films. So for a matte painter, it's almost the same. The only difference being that cinematics are full CG productions, similar technically to films like *Shrek* or what Pixar does. Everything is created through 3D software and the matte painting works to be part of that.

Newman: What values have you taken from working on film projects (like *Star Wars: Episode II* and the *Lord of the Rings* movies) and incorporated into your game pieces for Atari and Ubisoft?

Raynault: I think one of the good things learned while working on these big films is the ability to create photorealistic images, yet stylized with a touch of fantasy in it. Finding this balance is always a challenge and is more and more in demand in game cinematics. So technically it means to be able to mix painting skills with a dose of CG and photographic knowledge. Working on these films also lets your eyes see and record beautiful D.O.P. [Director of Photography] work as you sit down in those dailies seeing pieces of the film over and over. In our field you have to literally "eat" as much beautiful and impactful imagery as you can. The more photographic and filmic knowledge you accumulate, the better you are at judging your own work. And that is just one more opportunity!

Newman: Describe the communication between you and the team that will be designing animation or action over the scenes you have created for a game cinematic (cut-scene). Could the direction have taken any lessons from the film industry?

Raynault: Yes, I think there is still a lot to be learned by the cinematic people. But it's not necessarily from me! It seems that the standard in these teams is to hire fresh-out-of-school CG artists, which is totally valid, but unfortunately there is definitely a lack of movie-making knowledge in the equation. To me, if you want to create a nice short film before your video game or in the cut-scenes, you have to insufflate as much movie language as you can in it. This is valid in the art direction side of it, but also in the design of the cameras, use of lenses, and so on. I think it means hiring live action directors and art director to pair with CG people. To me, that is the ideal way you create rich collaborative teams.

Newman: What's your workflow like? How long does a piece usually take to finish?

Raynault: A matte painting [MP] for a film usually takes around two to three weeks of work. I usually start with some rough concepts and sketches and once it is approved, I move forward to create the final piece using whatever techniques and cheats to speed up the process. If it's a cityscape type of MP, I will use a 3D software to model basic geometry, texture it, and light it to give me a base image. From there, I will use painting and photographic techniques in Photoshop. This is where most of the important work happens. Once I have a satisfying image, it will either be projected back on 3D geometry to allow a camera move and parallax, or it will go straight to compositing if, for example, it's a lock off camera with foreground live action to be added in front.

Newman: What are the advantages of working digitally as opposed to creating a hand-made piece of art? How has technology affected your quality over the years?

Raynault: It is now impossible to achieve a matte painting without the use of the computer. The expectations now are way higher than they were twenty years ago. Audience can detect easily if a background looks painterly. That is why a final matte painting nowadays, even though it has been created with some painting techniques, contains no visible brush strokes. It became sort of a "created" photograph more than a painting, and that's why it has to be done digitally.

Newman: When trying to create a more cinematic game, what kinds of elements do you think need to be present in the artistic design to give it that kind of scope?

Raynault: The key elements to me are lighting, mood, and camera design. Designing live-action-like camera moves, choosing the right lenses, and creating interesting composition is a really big challenge in video games. And of course, establishing great direction of photography and replicating filmic lighting effect adds a lot to the look of game. The more you can get away from the perfectness of CG, the closer you'll get to a cinematic look!

Newman: You've managed to achieve a great standard in matte painting. What have been some of the better pieces of advice you have gotten over the years regarding working as an artist?

Raynault: In matte painting, one of the things you learn early on is that even though you are the creator of nice noticeable film background, it is not *your* art. You are part of a team trying to achieve a look for a film. Ultimately, you work for a director's visions and you achieve it within a group of people. It is learning to separate your own art creation from your job. It is still really fun to be a matte painter but it has nothing to do with being a painter.

Newman: What advice of your own do you have for art students wanting to work in the video game industry?

Raynault: Well, I am maybe not the right person to answers this, as my main field is the movie industry. But if, like in my case, you want to be involved in the image creation side of your industry, I would suggest trying to put together the best portfolio you can, containing traditional art pieces as well as digital art. The more you show your education is complete, and that you have explored many paths in art, the better it is. The students that have impressed me over the years were always the one that managed to present movie-like shots in their portfolio, achieving photorealistic and highly stylized looks with challenging concepts and strong art direction. Also, I would be careful with these eight-month CG school programs that guarantee you a job in the industry. They are not necessarily bad, but I think they need to be preceded and combined with more traditional education.

7

CINEMATOGRAPHY FOR GAMES

The term "cinematography" was created in the film industry to describe the process of creating images on film; as the use of film has diminished somewhat with the widespread availability of digital video and high definition formats, the term "cinematography" has expanded. Now it is a generic term encompassing all aspects of camera work, including the creative aspects involved with making aesthetically pleasing images and the technical aspects involved with using cameras, lights, and other equipment.

Cinematography has been around for a very long time with many influential directors and camera operators, but the field has changed very little—even with the current trend of using digital/high-definition digital mediums. Though cinematography is usually thought of as the elements that constitute the composition and style of a movie, it can also incorporate lighting techniques, camera movement, and even postproduction methods for creating the look that the director or cinematographer (usually a camera operator with lots of experience) is going for.

Though most techniques were designed for shooting movies, the visual elements of using basic cinematography techniques can also be applied to video games; both are visual mediums and both involve style, movement, and composition. When discussing the various elements of cinematography, most filmmakers refer to the work of Joseph V. Mascelli and his written work regarding the field (check out the seminal *The Five C's of Cinematography*, Silman-James Press, 1998).

7.1   Five C's of Cinematography

Though Mascelli wrote his book more than forty years ago, the basic principles he laid out still apply to visual mediums today. He came to the conclusion that the creative decisions made when shooting a film revolved around what he called the "five C's of cinematography." These C's include: camera angles, continuity, cutting, close-ups, and composition.

The use of creative camera angles in the video game process can be as easy as shifting the perspective of the gamer from first person to third person or as complicated as involving multiple camera angles from various viewpoints. Either way, the choice of camera angle can affect the atmosphere of the game, the intent and meaning the designer intended for the game, and even the depth/feel of the level/scene. A basic example of this would be using a low camera angle to represent the point of view of an insect protagonist. From this angle, everything would tower over the insect and create the feeling of vulnerability. Questions that a producer should be asking when determining the camera angles to use include, "What feeling/point-of-view do we want to create for the gamer?" and "What is the context of the scene?"

One of the major advantages a game cinematographer has over a film cinematographer is the actual "camera". Because a physical camera has size, it cannot be placed just anywhere within a scene. This limits the types of shots that can be achieved. In the gaming world, the camera has no size but is simply a point of view, so the camera can be placed literally anywhere within the shot. This can be used to achieve a level of shots and scenes that have never been seen or used in the film industry and can add great cinematic depth to the project.

Considering the context of a level or scene is a great way to make technical decisions regarding game cinematography (and maybe should be the sixth "C"). For instance, if your protagonist has just been in a helicopter crash and is trying to crawl from the wreckage, a wobbly/skewed camera angle could represent the disorientation and dizziness the character would be experiencing. Being consistent in the game with the use of creative camera angles helps keep the game on point with continuity.

Call of Duty 4: Modern Warfare includes many instances of point-of-view camera work. Reproduced by permission of Activision. All rights reserved.

The continuity aspect of cinematography involves keeping a consistent tone throughout the production. Though it can be thought of as limiting, continuity can be maintained while using a variety of camera angles and composition. Think of it as being consistent with the scene rather than consistent (or one-track) throughout the production. A lack of continuity with cameras creates gamer confusion and diminishes the overall production value of a game. It's important that the look and feel of a game remains consistent so that gamers will become immersed and enjoy a cinematic experience when playing. This can be achieved by staying with the "line of action", or the direction in which the game play will be heading.

Because the placement of the camera will be engineered during production, it is necessary to include notes about each level regarding the camera work. The notes should include the context of the level, any key creative decisions regarding the look and feel of the scene, and list any changes that should occur there.

In the film industry, the term "cutting" usually refers to the post-production aspect of editing. A film editor can get involved with a movie while it is still in production—mostly to insure that continuity is taking place and that the finished footage will have the necessary shots to cut a finished version of the film. Though this may be a less pertinent aspect of game cinematography, you can think of cutting in the game industry as editing as you go. Once you have a previsualization of what the level/scene should look like, you can then make the decisions regarding the other elements of game cinematography that will essentially "cut" the scene to look the way intended, then implement these decisions in production. Again, as most of these decisions will have been made in pre-production (with the script and storyboarding processes), the engineers will already have a plan to implement in level design.

The last two C's of cinematography involve framing. "Framing" a scene basically means the manner in which you position the camera and the proportions of the objects that are within the frame. The use of close-ups is one of the key ways to frame a scene. Another method of accomplishing this is to use the Rule of Thirds (discussed later) and the creative use of different kinds of shots to create variation within the continuity of the game.

Making sure to include true close-ups is very important in the film industry, as this is usually the method of choice for relaying intense emotion from the character (nothing beats a good close-up of the character's expression). Close-ups are also important to use when identifying key props or items in a scene. Though this approach might work only in certain gaming situations or cut-scenes, it is still a powerful way to illustrate the emotion of a scene, the personality of a character, or a key element of the story.

Development Tip

 Filmmakers use many names for the different styles of framing a shot. These include: extreme close-up, medium close-up, full close-up, wide close-up, close shot, medium close shot, medium shot, medium full shot, and full shot. Becoming familiar with these terms can help when making notes about your camera position. For instance, if you're reviewing a cut-scene that isn't working due to a lack of suspense, you might suggest doing it again from a low angle with a medium shot to get the look you want.

The *Far Cry* games from UbiSoft love the use of creative shots and close-ups. Reproduced by permission of UbiSoft. All rights reserved.

The final C that Mascelli spoke of is composition, which is the placement of the individual items/people within the shot. There are several approaches for achieving good composition, but most use the principal of importance: that is, the more important the item/person, the bigger it is in the shot. Alfred Hitchcock used a similar strategy for his camera work by stating, "The size of an object in the frame should equal its importance in the story at the moment." Cinematographers also believe that certain positions within a frame have more importance than others. This is usually called the Rule of Thirds.

7.2   Rule of Thirds

The Rule of Thirds (sometimes called the Rule of Three) is the basic technique of dividing an image into nine equal parts by imagining two equally dividing horizontal lines and two equally dividing vertical lines crossing the frame.

The four places where the vertical and horizontal lines cross are thought of as key positions for items within the frame. The use of this rule creates an image that is aesthetically better to the eye and naturally draws attention to that area of the frame. This technique has also been used as a way to misdirect a viewer; if the gamer is focused on the prop or person in the center of the screen, he or she can be led to believe that that item is the major area of importance rather than, say, a background item. This can add a sense of ambiguity or mystery to a scene.

Rule of Thirds diagram. The places where the lines intersect on the screen (in this case, the game *Saboteur*) are the locations that the human eye is most drawn to. Reproduced by permission of Pandemic Studios. All rights reserved.

7.3 Achieving the Look

When you visualize the way your game looks in your mind, is it in color or black-and-white? It is sharp or grainy? How about the use of color; do you think of the scenes in bright pastels or in muted monochromatic colors? What about lighting? Is everything brightly lit or shrouded in shadows? These are some of the major questions you must ask and discuss with the creative director to get the look you desire within the game.

Saboteur by Pandemic/EA illustrates the use of a black-and-white color scheme, as well as noir-style lighting to achieve a darker, older style. Reproduced by permission of Pandemic Studios. All rights reserved.

Think of the early concept art that you developed in preproduction as your primary means to locking down the style you want to achieve. When reviewing the design of backgrounds and characters, look at the individual elements within the piece. It's important to be able to answer the question "Why?" when an artist wants to know what does or does not work within a concept art piece. Even in the film industry, a look is often determined by the artwork (even when the art is applied as an effect in postproduction). The film *Three Kings* featured a simple bleach bypass process when developing the film that added the element of harsh lighting, intensity, and frenetic movement in the movie. This was completely engineered in postproduction, but was conceived from the film's onset. This is the mindset and process that must be followed when crating a cinematic game: conceive the look, design the look, then implement the look.

Another consideration that affects the look of your game is the choice of lenses that the virtual camera will use. Your designers must discuss this issue: How much of the world around the game character do you want the gamer to see? Good cinematographers use certain lenses to achieve certain styles in a shot. For instance, because of the extreme depth of field used in most video productions, most documentaries have a very "live" look to them. As most of the frame is in focus during video production, this means that the action being shot will seem real. After all, this is how the human eye works—we look at something and we see it in focus. In the film industry, this has become one of the major factors that determine whether a digital video (or high-definition [HD] video) production has a "film look". Most film cameras use lenses with a limited depth of field (meaning that a certain degree of the background will be out of focus), so digital video DV/HD productions have started limiting the focus within frame as a means to mimic shooting with film. This technique can also be applied to a game.

Let's say you are developing an FPS that takes place in the Iraq conflict. By keeping the entire frame in focus and using a jerky camera style, the game have a definite live feel—much like a documentary. Conversely, a great cut-scene for the same game illustrating a grand panoramic shot of the entire aftermath of the battleground would be done with a degree of slow, smooth camera movement coupled with the use of limited focus for distant objects. The use of focus/blur is yet another key way that cinematography can be used within the game to achieve a cinematic look.

The look of the game can also be affected by any effect that has been used in conjunction with the camera style. For instance, a level that takes place in the desert can have the effect of heat waves/ripples rising off metal objects. A character when struck by a bullet or fist can suddenly cause the scene to shift out of focus or become dimly lit as the character falls into unconsciousness.

Ubisoft's *Assassin's Creed* features the use of many virtual camera lenses. Reproduced by permission of UbiSoft. All rights reserved.

You can also think of adding effects much like a film cinematographer would think about using filters on a camera.

Think about some of the looks that are achieved with some of the most popular filters—color, polarizing, and neutral density—and how that look could be applied to your game. Mimicking the application of a lens filter can add cinematic depth to the visuals of the level.

7.4 Lighting in Games

Though part of the look of the game, lighting also refers to the technical aspects of cinematography. This includes the positioning of light, the intensity of the light being used, the placement of shadows, and the effect that the light will have upon the camera. Most of these elements can also be dealt with during the concept phase of getting the art department on point early on, but some of these must be also be thought of in a technical manner. For instance, when a character looks directly at the sun, can you still see other things around him or her, or does the sun blind the character? Maybe the sun creates a sort of lens flare on the camera.

Perhaps light will be a technical feature that's intended to affect the gamer during game play. For instance, in the game *Elder Scrolls IV: Oblivion*, most locations are far too dark to explore without the use of a "light spell" or flashlight. In the case of this game, the designers have made the lighting a game play element.

Lighting is also one of the ways that the game designer can affect the mood of the level. The use of a lot of shadows and limited visibility is a great way to make a game seem eerie or build tension. This is a staple of conventional horror games like *Silent Hill* and *Resident Evil*. Conversely, a lot of light can add a very sterile look to the scene. Many of the accomplished role playing

Development Tip

The American Society of Cinematographers often has great information about the use of various filters on camera and lights, as well as cinematography techniques to achieve certain cinematic looks on their Web site. Check them out at http://www.theasc.com.

A typical dark dungeon in *Elder Scrolls IV: Oblivion*. The Elder Scrolls IV: Oblivion® © 2006 Bethesda Softworks LLC, a ZeniMax Media company. All rights reserved.

games have made a fine art out of the use of dark levels. One of the oldest methods for lighting in the film industry revolves around the concept of "three-point lighting".

Three-point lighting is the most basic way of shooting a scene in the film industry; it refers to setting up three lights on the set: key light, fill light, and back light. The key light is in front of the action and illuminates the major elements of the scene. Think of it as the spotlight that is hitting the main character or object in the scene. It is usually the brightest light used and sets the tone (usually by intensity) of the lighting scene. In a game, the key light is probably the omnipresent light set at a distance of infinity that illuminates everything evenly. The remaining lights are used primarily for mood.

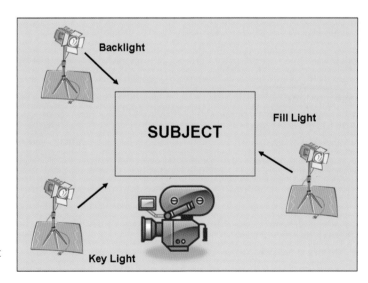

An example of three-point lighting.

The fill light hits the front and side spots of the frame that the key light does not. Typically, it is not as bright as the key light and is used to draw attention to any detail that is missed by the key light. Most cinematographers use this light to complement the key light (sometimes it is entirely omitted, but then it would only be two-point lighting).

The back light, as you would expect, is placed behind the items in the scene to create a degree of "rim light" around the subjects. The back light can be adjusted to either blend an object into a scene or separate/highlight the object. The way the back light is used is an aesthetic choice and can be manipulated to achieve the mood and look you want.

Sam Fisher, the protagonist of Ubisoft's *Splinter* Cell series, blends in well with his surroundings—an example of low back light. Reproduced by permission of UbiSoft. All rights reserved.

Though the use of three-point lighting is a fundamentally basic style in filmmaking, it can make a great jumping-off point for other styles of lighting. Start with this type of lighting, then adjust the light positioning, or quantity/intensity of lights to get the look you are trying to achieve. Because most games are in 3D, lighting a room or area in a game is quite different than lighting the set in a film. There will be situations therein that a movie's gaffer or cinematographer could only dream of. Attention must be paid to the spaces/places that normally would not be in the field of vision of a film viewer and treated with equal gravity in order to maintain consistency and continuity.

7.5 Camera Movement

Another key element in cinematography is the use of camera movement. For a physical camera, this means performing dolly and crane moves, panning and tilting the camera, and arranging the set to accommodate the movement (sometimes called "blocking" or "staging"). All of these movements can be accomplished within a game as well.

"Dolly moves" refer to the use of a physical dolly to move the camera along a set of tracks horizontally. Though a practical camera is limited to a set path, the dolly move on a virtual camera can weave and bob through a crowd, go through walls, or zoom in quickly on a specific object. A "crane move" also refers to a piece of filmmaking equipment. A crane moves a camera up and down, usually without a tilt. Just like the dolly moves, a game is not limited by where or how the camera gets from Point A to Point B while executing a crane move.

The use of a moving camera can add to the excitement of a game by keeping the action in frame. Camera movement can also be used to shift the attention of the gamer from one area to another; a simple way to do this would be the use of panning and/or tilting. "Panning" refers to the horizontal view of a stationary camera that moves from one spot in the scene to another. "Tilting" refers to doing the same thing vertically. In most games, the use of pan and tilt is usually implemented by incorporating the changing views into the point of view (POV) of the game character; in other words, the scene changes horizontally and vertically when the character looks around the level.

Once you have figured out the camera moves that you want to include within the scene or game level, you must figure out the positioning of the individual items/characters within the shot. Are they moving, too, or will they be static? Which elements in the shot are of higher importance? These are the questions that need to be asked when designing the level or cut-scene. One of the techniques for figuring out the individual elements of camera movement and placement in the film industry involves a process known as "previsualization". This can be as simple as storyboarding the level, or using a previsualization program.

Keep in mind, too, that cameras can be used within games in ways that filmmakers could never achieve. You can attach cameras to characters, shoot through solid objects, and get POV shots that would be impossible with a practical camera. This is one of the strengths and unique aspects of a video game and should be used as much as possible.

7.6   Staging

The best way to think of staging is to go back to the rule used by Hitchcock. Staging is basically how you arrange the characters and props within the scene. Again, the relationship of the asset in the frame can be based upon importance, or simply be a product of necessity (for example, a rock is placed in the forefront of the

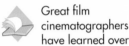

Development Tip

Great film cinematographers have learned over the years that the combination of a dolly/crane move with a pan/tilt adds great dimension to the scene. This dynamic use of the camera can give a project cinematic depth and add to the production value of the finished game.

Development Tip

One of the widely used previsualization programs in the film industry is called FrameForge 3D Studio. You can download a demo version of the program on the program's official Web site: http://www.frameforge3d.com.

scene, because this is a place where the protagonist can take cover). Once you have placed everything within the level, natural areas or zones will emerge.

The various zones provide natural boundaries for the placement of cameras. For instance, if you recognize that the level can be divided into four clear areas, a static camera can be placed in each of these; this way, when the gamer has finished clearing a zone, the POV can shift to the camera placed in the next zone as the gamer enters that area. Good staging should be used in conjunction with blocking, applying the rule of three, and the sound techniques of framing discussed previously.

7.7 Blocking

"Blocking" is the process of mapping out the movement of assets within the frame. For instance, a typical FPS features levels where the protagonist enters the scene and then must cross an area of space to complete the level. This involves the protagonist moving; though the movement of the protagonist can be predicted to a certain extent (paths will be limited by placed obstacles and boundaries), the interactivity of the gamer should be preserved by presenting multiple paths. To this end, the placement of props and obstacles in the scene determine the blocking of the main game character.

In addition to the protagonist, there can also be nonplayer characters (NPCs) moving within a scene. Going back to the FPS example, as the protagonist crosses the main area, there will be opposing forces moving to stop the protagonist and engage the gamer. Because these will be controlled by the game itself, the blocking of NPCs can definitely be planned. A certain degree of variation can be included through the use of artificial intelligence, but again, the movement will be limited to a degree by obstacles and boundaries.

The Master Chief of *Halo 3* attempts to cross the room.

Development Tip

For detailed ways to code and implement some of the cinematography concepts of this chapter, consider picking up *Real-Time Cinematography for Games* by Brian Hawkins (Charles River Media, 2005). The book lays out many of the ways to engineer cinematography techniques into your game.

Bruce Block

The detailed planning of blocking within a level will help the engineering department and technical director with level design and coding. Typically, the use of blocking techniques is coupled with creative staging for dramatic effect. When used correctly, these rules of good cinematography add a huge cinematic impact to your game.

Interview: Bruce Block, Author of *The Visual Story*

Bruce Block has served as a producer, director or creative consultant on feature films, television shows, commercials, animated films, computer games, and IMAX movies. His feature film credits include: *The Holiday, Something's Gotta Give, Stuart Little, As Good As It Gets, The Parent Trap* and *America's Sweethearts*.

Mr. Block is the author of *The Visual Story*, which is used throughout the world as the standard text for understanding the relationship between story and visual structure. He also teaches visual structure at USC's School of Cinematic Arts and gives seminars at animation studios, film schools, and interactive game companies.

Newman: In your book *The Visual Story*, you talk about "controlling pictures". Give a quick version of what the workflow would be in creating controlled visual art.

Block: First, you have to answer these questions:

1. What's the story conflict? Not the plot, but the conflict.
2. Who are the characters?
3. What's the story genre?
4. What's the story theme or premise?
5. What is the point of view? Point of view means how does the picture maker want the audience to feel about the subject? (Example: The Vietnam War was: dangerous; funny; romantic; a nightmare).
6. Where does the story take place? What natural visual components exist in that location?

Now, based on your point of view, research the story and locations. Create or find photographs, drawings, paintings, written material, or movies that suggest various visual approaches. What visual ideas in other people's work communicate the point of view that you have in mind? This isn't stealing; this is research. If you have to make a movie about the Civil War, you research it because you don't have any firsthand knowledge of the Civil War. If you're doing a movie about contemporary New York, you will visit the city, take pictures, and perhaps get photo books about the city full of pictures taken by other people. It's likely that all of the artists who came before you had some great ideas about the visual side of New York that you can use for inspiration. If you don't want to use research, create concept art yourself. Do this intuitively. What visuals feel right to you? Free associate and create new pictures, sculptures, photos, and so on that communicate your point of view.

Analyze the story or script to see how it's structured. You must be able to define the conflict and see where it gains story conflict intensity. As I suggest in my book, create graphs that show the story and visual structure. Use the principle of contrast and affinity to give your pictures a visual structure that communicates your point of view and parallels the story conflict.

Newman: How does the visual structure of games differ from that of film?
Block: The visual structure of a motion picture film is predetermined. The film is the same viewing experience for every audience who has no control of any aspect of the presentation. In a video game, the player can rearrange the story structure and the visual components. The game can be a different story and a different visual experience each time it's played, whereas the film will always be the same.

Newman: How can games take a cue from film structure?
Block: Film's story and visual structure are critical to good storytelling. Every story (no matter how short or long) has an exposition, a conflict, and a resolution. Something as simple as a joke has all three of these story elements, as does a short story, a graphic novel, a traditional novel, or a movie (of any length). A game must also have these elements. The exposition is the information needed to begin; the game conflict is solving the puzzle, eradicating the enemy, finding something, saving something, escaping from somewhere, and so on; the resolution in a game is success or failure.

In film, when a writer, director, production designer, or cinematographer structures the visuals, certain basic questions must be answered: What is the overall mood? What emotions should the audience feel and when should they feel them? What is the conflict in the story and how can the visual structure make that conflict evident? How can the story's intensifying conflict be paralleled by the visual structure? How can the story be made visually cinematic? A film crew is divided into departments (writing, acting, casting, directing, camera, lighting, set design, costumes, props, special effects, sound effects, and music) so that every area can be examined, controlled, and used to help tell the story, set the mood, and communicate the point of view.

Newman: What elements do you look for in a visually strong movie?

Block: I look for a controlled use of the basic visual components as they are outlined in my book. These components are space, line, shape, color, tone, movement, and rhythm. These same components are the visual building blocks of any pictorial art form, including games. Specifically, what movies do I consider to be visually strong? Everyone has a different list, but the great visual movies are the ones you can remember long after you've seen them. If you must have an actual list, please read my book, because it uses examples from movies with strong visuals only.

Newman: Given the interactivity of games, how do you approach the challenge of creating a strong narrative visually, because the timeline of events in a game can be in flux?

Block: You can't create a visual narrative. You can use visuals to support a narrative that tells a story but visual components by themselves can't tell a story. Visuals can create a mood or evoke an emotional response or create visual intensity but I don't think pure visuals can tell a specific story. An actor walking around without talking doesn't qualify as a narrative visual. Graphic novels without words tell a story but they are very representative drawings. A wordless graphic novel is a pantomime, so we still rely on facial expression, body language, and anthropomorphic symbols to tell stories. An interactive game, no matter how nonlinear, still has a beginning and an end. As the player plays the game, events can occur based on game play, not on a scripted plan. It is still critical to any structure that there be a build towards the end or at least structural variety so that the game play remains visually interesting. A flexible timeline or a game player's random access to events cannot be an excuse to ignore visual structure.

Classically, the most intense part of a conflict is the climax where the conflict ends. In some video games, the final battle is the most intense, or the final puzzle is the most complicated, or the last race is the most difficult. No one wants to play a game where the most difficult stuff is first and then everything gets progressively easier. Each level of a video game is more difficult or exciting so that the structure builds in conflict intensity. Programmers must plan for the interactivity and nonlinear play that occurs in games. If the sequence of scenes (or events) is designed as A-B-C-D-E-F, the game designer can't ignore the fact that the player might encounter the scenes in a different order like: F-A-E-C-B-D. No matter how the player encounters the scenes, the designer must create a flexible structural plan. If the scenes are encountered out of order (and F is the most intense scene), predetermining and locking the visual design of the scenes won't work. Because the player can change the scene (or event) order, that player can easily encounter the scenes in any structural order. The scenes have to be programmed with flexibility so that an intensifying structural experience can be had no matter how the scenes are encountered. Even if a player returns to a scene that has been "completed", it should look different based on where else the player has gone and where the player is now positioned in the overall visual structure.

In global multiplayer games, visual variety in the environments is critical to keeping the game interesting. Different "universes" will be easier or more difficult to encounter based not only on who is there but also by how it's visually designed. Should an explosion occurring on Level 1 look like an explosion that occurs on Level 20? Probably not. How the explosions can differ depends on the visual structure that is created based on the story and point of view.

Newman: With cinematography now becoming a serious subject in the game industry, describe the impact that choice of framing and lighting can have on a scene.

Block: Cinematography and lighting have a huge impact on visual structure. Most interactive games leave framing choices to the player. The game designer does have certain controls like lens choice and limits that can be placed on the camera's mobility, but camera angle is usually not controlled by the designer. Lighting can be controlled by the designer (time of day, existing light sources, and so on) or the player (carrying flashlights, torches, finding light switches, and so on). A good cinematographer has a huge range of styles that can be used: a film-noir style, sitcom style, horror-film style, overexposure, contrasting lighting, hard lighting, soft lighting, lighting direction, color of light, intensity of light, one light source or multiple light sources, and so on.

A game designer who is concerned with camera angle and lighting should pick ten classic films and run them with the sound off and study the lighting. The designer should also take some classes in photographic lighting styles. Camera and lighting are very sophisticated cinematic techniques that elevate visual structure. In film and television, experienced cinematographers create extraordinary moods and visual styles with lighting, but it takes a lot of experimenting and practice. A designer that thinks lighting is only there to see the action is missing a key element in visual structure.

Newman: Most games are being developed today with a well-defined story and characters, but the theme is usually murky at best. What's the process concerning the use of space and color to help define a theme?

Block: The theme of most games seems to be: "Getting killed is a bad thing" or "Do this because it's fun or exciting". Generally speaking, deep space is more dramatic than flat space, because deep space creates visual contrasts. So if deep is dramatic, it can be used to define themes that are dramatic or intense. Flat space can also be dramatic, but it needs other visual component contrasts to gain the needed visual intensity. Remember that space is going to be a general backdrop behind the story to help define mood and support the intensity of the conflict. Space doesn't have the ability to get as specific as color.

Color has three "control knobs": hue, brightness, and saturation, which allows a wide range of color choices. Color can communicate to an audience more specifically than space. Like any visual component, meanings can be assigned to a color. Color already has a lot of stereotypic meanings that can communicate a theme: for example, bright saturated colors are happy; saturated red can communicate danger or passion; desaturated blue can show depression. Again, these are hokey stereotypes, as any color can be made to communicate almost anything.

Newman: When one reads a story or watches a movie, you can always tell when the writer has a great rhythm—the story just flows and the characters are all well-defined. What sort of "checklist" could a game designer use to determine whether good rhythm is present in the game's visual style?

Block: The most important factor in rhythm of a game, I think, is intuitive play. A game can be difficult to win, but its rhythm must feel intuitive. I don't think a player will get involved in a game that doesn't have an intuitive rhythmic feel to the overall play. Visual rhythm is based on controlling a picture's linear motif. You can find the linear motif of a picture by reducing it to lines. If you reduced your entire game to a series of pictures of lines (curved, straight, horizontal, vertical, and diagonal), how would they stack up in terms of structure?

The easiest way to see the linear motif is by removing the color and then increasing the contrast of the picture until there's nothing left but black and white. That remaining harsh, contrasty image is the linear motif, which reveals the visual rhythm. When we look at any picture, we might describe the visual rhythm as calm, jumpy, agitated, soothing, mellow, chaotic, slow, or fast. All of those descriptive words are how we feel emotionally about the linear motif. As a game is a series of pictures, how does this series of linear motifs (the pictures) reveal contrast or affinity? In my book, there's an entire chapter devoted to finding linear motif and understanding how to control it structurally. Visual rhythm is also created by editing or cutting from one shot to another. Most games tend to be a single, endless shot, so editing isn't usually a factor in a computer game.

8

PRODUCER

In the film and game industries, the job title "producer" can mean a lot of different things. It all depends on the context of the position and the medium in use. Regardless of these two factors, however, there is a definite skill set involved with working as a producer and being successful. Good management skills, experience working with people, and broad knowledge of the industry is essential for any type of longevity in either film or game.

Though it may seem that the game industry would not have much to learn from this particular film position with regard to making a cinematic game, it is the best practices of top-notch producers that bring in epic productions on time and on budget. One of the first credits you see in any film or game is that of a producer, so we know it must be an important job. But what does a producer actually do?

8.1   Job Description

The simplest description of a film or game producer is the human bridge between the management (the money) and the talent. A typical day for a game producer consists of keeping up with scheduling, tracking assets and milestones, keeping the production team on track and free of distractions, attending numerous meetings, and basically taking on any task that seems to miss falling in the laps of everyone else on the team. The challenges involved with planning and executing the production of a game can be daunting.

In the film industry, the position is much the same—lots of scheduling and budgeting—but the position usually includes many of the artistic decisions that are usually associated with a game's creative director. A film producer often has a major say in casting for certain roles, what the overall "message" of a film will be (sometimes this is reflected in the producer's choice of director), and where the film will be shot. But before we apply some of the best practices of the film producer to the game development model, let's take a closer look at what a game producer actually does.

Depending on the relationship between the developer and the publisher, there can be several different types of producers working on a production.

8.2   Types of Producers in the Game Industry

A typical game studio (or developer) has several different producers working on the payroll. Usually, this can be upwards of four to ten producers working on any given project. The entry-level position is usually called an "associate producer" or sometimes an "assistant producer"—here, I'll use "AP" to refer to either title. These individuals are the ground-level grunts of the producer team. They deal with the employees of the development team on a daily basis, deal with issues within the team, and are usually responsible for a specific aspect of development, such as sound design, coding, or animation. Most development teams have several APs working within the production. The AP also coordinates communication between quality assurance and production and adjusts the daily schedule to reflect any changes that are occurring in production.

In most cases, APs are assisted in the daily grind of grunt work by production assistants (PAs) or interns assigned to the team. In a best-case scenario, a good PA will take some of the workload off the AP and assist with the minutia of the studio routine—in a worst-case scenario, the PA will know nothing of game development and will become one more thing that the AP will have to manage. As most APs come from the world of production assistants and quality assurance personnel, it becomes an essential task of the studio to train and bring up this natural source of internal talent.

A typical game, such as Propaganda Games' *Turok*, has many producers on the payroll. Reproduced by permission of Disney Interactive. All rights reserved.

The next rung on the producer ladder is a title that is seen quite a bit in the film world: the line producer. A line producer is usually the go-to person when it comes to budget. Much like the film position, he or she spends the work day knee-deep in the production team overseeing the nuts and bolts of production to make sure that the project is finished on time and on budget. Line producers typically report to the studio heads and work somewhat outside the producer chain of command. Think of LPs as the accountant of the development team.

Making the move to full-blown producer is the next step in the producer's career path. There are two types of producers—those who work for the publisher and those who work for the developer/studio. Those who work for the publisher are responsible for getting the game produced. They answer directly to the publisher and ultimately accept the largest part of the accolades or criticisms associated with the finished game. The workload for this type of producer is the stuff of nightmares. In addition to the usual full plate of meetings, this type of producer must keep up on all the daily reports coming in, getting those same reports out to the appropriate people within the studio and at the publisher, and constantly evaluating the current project to make sure that all workflow is streamlined and working with cohesion.

Producers who work for an outside developer have similar roles, but ultimately are responsible for maintaining good relations with the publisher. Usually the publisher has producers on the studio site working as well, but the tasks remain the same with regard to scheduling, management, and communication. In addition to the responsibilities involved with maintaining the contract with the publisher, a developer-level producer also must report to the studio heads the current state of affairs using daily delta reports to ensure that internal problems remain internal.

Producers are also involved with the day-to-day operations of the team, such as resolving conflicts that arise, dealing with dependencies, and working with outside contractors to make sure that deliverables are coming in on schedule (as well as payments going out in a timely manner). The key to being a successful producer is organization and communication.

Sometimes, a game project will also have an executive producer. This position might be in place of a creative director, or working in conjunction with him or her. Usually, an executive producer is involved with the business side of things. Though creative input will be required of all producers, the executive producer is usually involved with the company on a larger scale; rather than dealing with specific titles or games, usually this kind of producer is the central figure associated with the brand or franchise game associated with the developer/publisher. Sometimes, this position can also be associated with dealing with the marketing and business doings of the developer/publisher. The traits of a highly successful executive producer include strong leadership abilities and communication, a complete understanding of what makes a successful game and how to market it, and competency at determining and managing risk.

A successful game like the *Lord of the Rings Online* employs many producers during development. The artwork appearing to the right is copyright protected and reproduced with permission. © 2008 Turbine, Inc. All rights reserved. This publication is in no way endorsed or sponsored by Turbine, Inc. or its licensors.

All of these producer positions are important and all of them have been associated with the film industry for decades. Now that we have identified the individual traits and skills of a producer, we can address how to improve them using the film producer as an example.

8.3   Honing Your Production Skills

I will discuss the particulars of the individual skill sets involved with production and producing; first, I'll talk about the things that define and hone a mediocre producer into a great producer. These include communication, professionalism, organization, and leadership.

Great communication is the hallmark of a great producer. The first step in being a great communicator is learning how to listen. The best approach to this is the concept of "active listening", or the process of focusing on the person speaking to you, and trying to understand the meaning and underlying reasons of what the speaker is trying to say. Only when you understand why the person is saying what they are will you be able to respond accurately and in accordance to what is being discussed. In addition to listening to the content of what is being said, it is also important to notice how the person is saying it. Is the speaker agitated? Nervous? Excited? Noticing these things helps place importance upon what is being discussed and allows you to place the conversation in proper perspective.

Sometimes listening means that you will be accepting criticism or suggestions that do not coincide with your own. The role of the producer is to make sure that a product is developed as well as humanly possible—this means examining all input that is provided. There will always be some level of truth to all criticism, and this truth will often have to be extracted from the editorial content of the suggestions being made. Once you have done that, take the criticism for what it is. Does it help? If so, implement it. If not, discard it and move on. Either way, communicating back and forth with your team will instill a sense of working as a team, help build consensus, and create respect within the workplace. Communication is the first step to developing professionalism in the workplace.

Being a professional producer means keeping your perspective and being objective when dealing with co-workers and problems in the workplace. This means not taking sides in arguments and conflicts, following through with correcting problems, maintaining discretion, and creating a sense of reliability. When the team realizes that you can always be trusted with solving a problem logically and discreetly, you will become privy to more of the underlying issues within the workplace. Though you may delegate some of the particulars of correcting problems to others, ultimately it should be you that becomes the "go-to" person when a crisis occurs.

The third hallmark of a great producer is organization. Mastering the nuances of great project management will assist you with this. As producing a movie can involve a vast array of logistics, film producers have relied upon quality film production software to help with this (such as Gorilla Pro, www.junglesoftware.com). Once again, the primary organization tools used in the game industry usually revolve around Microsoft Project, Microsoft Excel, the use of online internal sites (such as a wiki page or Perforce), and daily reporting. Once you have mastered the tools of the project management trade, it's a good idea to schedule desk time for yourself each day. Consider the time that you spend catching up on the logistics of development at your desk to be as important as meetings and time on the floor.

Development Tip

 Mind Tools (http://www.mindtools.com) offers great advice, instruction, and tests designed to improve interpersonal skills in the workplace. Visit their site to learn more about active listening, time management, stress management, and project planning.

Development Tip

One of the best ways to ensure your competency as a project manager is to become certified by the Project Management Institute (http://www.pmi.org). This will not only sharpen your management abilities, but will also be a great addition to your resume when searching for work as a producer. In the meantime, download a free copy of FreeMind (http://freemind.sourceforge.net/wiki/index.php/Main_Page) and get organized!

Perhaps the most underrated skill of the successful producer is that of leadership. It's the intangible trait that can define your longevity with a developer/publisher and your success with production. What makes a good leader? A good leader, in short, knows what he or she wants, gets things done, and inspires others to do the same. This means instilling a positive attitude in everyone (including yourself); empowering others to learn, grow, and accomplish; and being passionate about your work. It's amazing how much difference it can make to work in a positive, nurturing environment versus the alternative. People want to work for great leaders and great leaders want to work for the people. Honing this skill not only facilitates a smoother production cycle, but also gives you job security at the studio.

Once you have mastered the skills of a great producer, you can apply these talents to the development of a cinematic game. Let's take a look at how the development of a strong game concept can be achieved using a filmmaking skill set.

2K/BioWare's game *BioShock* is an example of a well-produced, cinematic game. Reproduced by permission of 2K Games. All rights reserved.

8.4 Cinematic Development

One of the first things that a film producer does in development/preproduction of a new movie is to break down the script. "Breaking down" the script essentially means making a logistics list of every element of production in order to set up a budget and schedule. When a script is broken down, you will have a detailed list of every location, character, prop, and so on within the script. There are several great reasons for including this process in game development, but the biggest will be to help determine whether the script will need to be rewritten. Are there too many locations/levels for the game's budget? Are there too many peripheral/unnecessary characters putting a strain on the workload of the artists? More than anything, breaking down the script is about honing the story so that it is the best possible draft and the one that will translate the story to the actual game.

Another great side benefit of breaking down the script involves taking a closer look at the locations that are to be used in the production. Are they dynamic enough? Do they make the game exciting and unique, as well as present a new challenge to the gamer? Will you be sending actual members of the production team to the locations featured to get a feel for the environment? This is yet another factor that can affect your schedule and budget. Make wise location choices. Great locations can be one of the factors that determine the game's success.

Ubisoft's *Assassins Creed* does a great job of depicting locations like ancient Jerusalem. Reproduced by permission of UbiSoft. All rights reserved.

Once you have a basic script breakdown (see the sample Script Breakdown in the Extras section of this book), you then need to ask whether the script is ready for production. If not, rewrites are in order—or the other logistics must be altered to accommodate the script (such as hiring new artists to take on the additional environments and characters). Breaking down the script also assists with identifying the major theme of the story and making sure that the script stays on subject. Often after a script has been honed to its best possible draft, it will still seem a little bit off. When this happens, producers/writers often use a technique known as getting script coverage.

"Script coverage" means sending out the script for review by various experts in the screenwriting industry. Once the person providing coverage has read the script, they will make extensive notes about the story, characters, plot, and so on. These notes can be helpful with getting your script on track. Having a great script finished, with all the logistics of the script breakdown planned in advance, will help minimize the risk associated with going into production with an unfinished story/game design.

8.5 Risk Management

As the primary task of the producer is to make sure that the game actually gets produced, it is imperative that the art of risk management is mastered. Risk management can basically be broken down into three steps: identifying the risks, prioritizing the risks, and then minimizing the risks.

Identifying all the risks involved with producing your game means getting together with every single department lead and discussing the potential problems involved therein. Risks can include problems with the development pipeline, lack of workstations, or even time. As these risks are singled out, they should be documented in detail for future reference. Identifying every risk associated with production will allow you be proactive in prevention of potential problems, as well as create a buffer in the budget and schedule to accommodate the possible occurrence of a problem. The risk assessment should focus on every aspect of development, including labor, cost, assets, time, dependencies, and so on.

Once all possible risks have been detailed, you must then prioritize them according to the potential impact that the issue will have upon production. Once the risks have all been listed per department by priority, you can then assign the major issues to leads so that they can put prevention measures in place. This is one way of minimizing risk in development.

There are other ways that risks can be avoided. These include creating a sound business plan, design, and prototype before going into formal production, creating a contingency fund in the game's budget, and planning as much as possible in preproduction so that the production will be as smooth as possible. Preproduction planning is one of the strongest assets that a game producer can take from the film producer (realizing of course that game producers are already involved with preproduction). In most movie productions, a producer will not even get a green light from the production company to proceed into production without an extensive and thorough preproduction phase.

8.6 Preproduction Planning

One of the considerations that come into play when planning the schedule for a film involves the shooting order that will occur. Films are most often shot with the individual scenes of a script out of sequence. This is done for many reasons. These reasons usually revolve around the availability of actors, the availability of certain locations, and sometimes the weather of a particular location (such as having scenes that take place during a snowstorm). When all the logistics are taken into consideration, the shooting order can then be made.

Once you have taken into account limiting factors such as availability, the shooting order is then constructed based upon priority or difficulty. If there is a particularly difficult scene to shoot, often the producer/director will schedule that scene first so that it isn't looming at the end of production. Finishing the hardest scene early in production means that the production crew can heave a collective sigh of relief when it is over and then move on to the easier scenes. This is a great philosophy when producing a game as well. Finishing a particularly challenging aspect of development early produces a sense of accomplishment with the dev team and can lay the ground work for producing an awesome early build. Of course, finishing the first scene means designing the first scene.

Ideally, the entire production will be designed during preproduction, but often a game is built before all the levels have been completely fleshed out. Again, by taking a cue from the film industry and finishing the entire production style and look during preproduction with proven production techniques (such as storyboarding, script reads, and so on), you will ensure a more consistent, quality production.

Games like UbiSoft's *Rainbow Six* series benefit from having a well developed book (*Rainbow Six* by Tom Clancy) to draw from. Reproduced by permission of UbiSoft. All rights reserved.

At any rate, once the shooting order is determined, there evolves a sort of pecking order as to what aspects of production must be finished first—or what cannot be produced until a preceding task is accomplished. These are usually called "dependencies" in the game industry. Figuring out the dependencies early in the process helps with making an accurate early schedule. An example of a dependency is that animators might not be able to begin making character models until the artists have drawn/designed them.

Another task that has to be tackled by the producer during film preproduction is the balancing of "above-the-line" and "below-the-line" talent. Above-the-line talent includes actors, voice-over actors, directors, and so on. Below-the-line is basically the crew. Though this may seem like a film-centric factor to take into account during production, it is an increasingly more prevalent concern in the game industry.

With games like Midway's *Stranglehold* being directed by John Woo or voice actors such as Michael Ironside (the voice of Ubisoft's *Tom Clancy's Splinter Cell* hero Sam Fisher) being cast for voiceover work, above-the-line budgets for games have increased significantly over the last five years. There's no denying that star power can increase the marketability of a game and the acquisition of name talent is at a current premium—but acquiring that kind of talent can take a large chunk out of your budget. There are several ways, though, that producers can minimize this cost.

The *Splinter Cell* series by Ubisoft features the voice work of actor Michael Ironside. Reproduced by permission of UbiSoft. All rights reserved.

The first way is through research: who is in between productions? Who hasn't worked in a while? Maybe a particular actor lives in the area or will be in the area, and will therefore be a lot cheaper to acquire. This is where your negotiation skills come into play. Learning how to negotiate, make the best possible deal, and get quality talent and team on your production ultimately is the job of the producer—and should all be done during preproduction to make sure that it all fits in the production budget.

8.7   Managing Money, Assets, and Time

As already discussed earlier in this chapter, it is one of the producer's primary tasks to work out the budget and schedule for a production. This task is usually shared during the production of a game between the creative director and the studio heads, as well as the publisher. One thing that the studio heads most likely will not help you with is actually managing all these things. Getting on track management-wise means having the proper tools to do your job. The major areas that must be addressed include scheduling, documenting, and tracking.

The major scheduling tools have been basically discussed in previous chapters: Microsoft Project, Microsoft Excel, and even Microsoft Outlook can be helpful when dealing with the sheer amount of required meeting time and face time. Nothing will make you as unproductive as having an outdated or messed-up schedule. Once again, the key to getting the most out of your workday will revolve around minimizing meeting overload and getting time on the floor to interact with the development team.

The documenting aspect of managing assets and reports is often the most overlooked in the world of the producer. It's important to establish regular work habits in regard to archiving assets, keeping reports flowing, and keeping up the schedule and budget. In addition to organizing your own workstation, it's important that many of the assets and reports used in development be available to the entire team; being privy to the current operations in the other various areas of the studio can be important on the floor and leads need easy access to those materials. This is usually achieved by having/hosting an online wiki page that every department can contribute to. By making subpages that focus on art, engineering, QA, and so on, you help the individual department leads make sure that their section is always up to date on the site. Ideally, the studio heads/producers should be able to go into the site at any given time and see what is happening in every department, as well as whether the production is on schedule and budget.

The easiest way to keep a tight schedule is to have regularly scheduled milestones; if the production is hitting the milestones on budget and schedule, the project will be on track. This is the easiest way for monitoring progress.

The second way that progress will be followed throughout the studio is through daily reporting. Sometimes called "daily delta reports", this system is used by most developers to track what has been accomplished on a daily basis. This task can be done on an individual basis throughout the development team, but usually it's done by section. Basically, each team member or lead sends in a daily email that lists all tasks finished that day, then a producer (or whoever has been assigned to handle this particular task) compiles the list into a department-by-department spreadsheet to turn in to the studio heads. This is an easy way to stay on top of what the team is getting done without taking up too much of your day to do it. Just keep in mind that the time the team is spending on reports is time they are not working on the game!

8.8   Postproduction

In addition to the challenges and complications that arise during preproduction and production of a film, it is also typically the job of the executive producer to find distribution for the finished movie. Although this is not usually a problem in the game industry—you most likely will not have gone into full-blown development without a deal in place—there's no denying that producers are often the ones pitching a game to the publisher and attempting to make the sell. But again, this is usually done before any production is done on the game.

During postproduction in the game industry, the game producer is usually more involved with making sure that localization is on point and working with the publisher to handle the various marketing duties involved with a new release. This includes the ad campaign, print campaign, getting media coverage, and attending conferences to promote the title. Hopefully, during production you will have created a great, cinematic trailer to promote with. Now is the time to unveil it and promote your game.

Games like Pandemic Studios' *Saboteur* make huge impacts at conferences prior to the game's release. Reproduced by permission of Pandemic Studios. All rights reserved.

Film producers have been promoting at film festivals for many years and have learned hard lessons there. Using these lessons, a basic set of rules for success at a game conference is the following:

1. *Take quality assets.* Make sure that you have great screen-shots, press kits, trailers, and demos for the conference—and make sure people see them.

2. *Bring swag.* Nothing draws people to your booth/area more than having free stuff to give them. Keep in mind that things you give away with the game's logo on it will go a long way towards putting free advertisement on the streets.

3. *Go to the parties.* Nothing makes a better presence or gets you farther than glad-handing at the parties. Schmoozing with media and making the game's presence known at the fun events gets you great press.

4. *Do some guerilla marketing.* Get posters up all over the place, get flyers into the goodie bags, and put postcards in the hands of everyone possible. It all adds up to making a big impression on the public.

5. *Try to speak at the conference.* Another way to get to a lot of people is to get a speaking gig there. Sometimes it's as easy as contacting the conference (just do it far in advance when they are still planning it).

Doing well at conferences is one of the "soft skills" that producers should all have inherently—and if they don't, they should be developing these skills, which go a long way when working with your public relations department.

Interview: Bob Sabiston, Founder of Flat Black Films

Bob Sabiston grew up in North Carolina and received his bachelors and masters degrees from the MIT Media Lab. He owns an animation company, Flat Black Films, headquartered in Austin, Texas, since 1993. He and his team of freelance animators produce some of the most eye-popping animation around. In addition to being the creative director of the company, Bob writes the software for all of their animated films. Their work includes the recent movies *Waking Life*, *A Scanner Darkly*, and *The Five Obstructions*. Also, Flat Black Films' own short films have been winning awards and breaking new ground in computer animation since 1988. These include *RoadHead* (1998), *Snack and Drink* (1999), *Beat Dedication* (1988), *Grinning Evil Death* (1991), and most recently, *The Even More Fun Trip* (2007).

Bob Sabiston

Newman: Your studio, Flat Black Films, usually has a team of animators/artists working on a project. How do you manage a group of individuals to stay within the artistic vision of the project? Describe the workflow in your studio.

Sabiston: Well, I try to manage the "artistic vision" of a project so that it can comfortably grow out of the collaboration between a group of good artists. I think that ultimately, what looks good is a good artist doing their work with the minimal interference possible. There is an expectation out there that something needs to look the same to hold together or appear cohesive. Really, I think it is just a matter of selectively using each person's very different styles. The vision is attained just by working daily with the same smallish group of people; it grows organically from that I think.

Newman: One of the challenges of working in the game industry is staying up on technology. Though game artists have laid the foundation for standardization within their field by using the same basic programs, programmers have yet to do so. What have been some of the challenges you have faced in the film industry with coping with technology?

Sabiston: We use our own software, which has a whole set of challenges all its own. But I face a similar problem simply with the release of new versions of the OS for the computers we use. For example, Mac OS X 10.5 (Leopard) broke my program. Now I have to go back into all that code, which I haven't worked on in a while, and figure out why. The transition from OS 9 to OS X was horrible too, but worth it of course. But it's sobering to think that I will have to keep my program alive, essentially, as time marches forth, by staying on top of changing API programming. Also, we move to HD and all of a sudden everything's getting bigger, which affects everyone in terms of needing more disk space, faster computers. But for us animators, drawing on these 1920×1080 screens, the temptation is now there to dive into an even greater level of detail. It's good, but it's bad, possibly akin to wanting to hear a vinyl album over a CD or mp3.

Newman: When you were working on the films *Waking Life* and *A Scanner Darkly*, you were in a position to collaborate with director Richard Linklater concerning the look of the films. More so than any other films, these films are closely related to games in that they are "real" but animated. Describe the artistic process of interpreting a director's vision and keeping the film cinematic rather than cartoon-like.

Sabiston: Well, our specific type of animation is "rotoscoping", which already has the benefit of being traced over live action, if you're looking for cinematic over cartoonish. But I think with *Waking Life* and *A Scanner Darkly*, I think we both had the same general idea of the look for each film. We were on the same page there, which helps. As far as process, regular meetings and reviews of artwork again just kind of naturally lead to a shared understanding for the look of something. *Scanner* was much more detailed, and was kind of the opposite of *Waking Life*, in that it maintained this single, consistent, very detailed style the whole way though the movie. Ultimately, I had little to do with how they ended up seeing that through. I think Rick, as well as the studio, panicked when they realized what an actually huge task that would be when compared to *Waking Life*.

Newman: Your particular brand of animation is unique in that you begin with living actors, then rotoscope over the top of the image. This is not unlike the use of motion capture in the game industry, then animating over the movements of the real actors. Have you found any particular methodology for directing actors that seems to translate the best into your projects?

Sabiston: Most of what I've directed, when we animate, has been documentary. So I'm just recording people being themselves and then picking that over for good moments. Although I agree that the rotoscoping process has much in common with motion capture, there's the hand-drawn aspect to rotoscoping. The artist does give the animation an emotion, an expressiveness, and individuality that motion capture doesn't really have. I think they both have good uses. The film *Beowulf*, for example, seemed like a pretty good use for the motion capture, whereas *Waking Life* wouldn't be too good done that way. Video games: it would be interesting to see one that really made good use of rotoscoping's advantages. I don't think it would be your typical game.

Newman: When translating emotion into a project, color and light can play a big part in establishing a desired mood. This can be particularly difficult when dealing with animation. What is your philosophy regarding the incorporation of light and color?

Sabiston: Because of the tracing aspect to our animation, we pick up most of our light effects from the video source. So in those instances, you'd just be facing the same lighting and color choices as a live-action filmmaker, with the exception that you know you have this second opportunity, during the animation, of changing things. On the other hand, you can also ignore all the video color and lighting and just do your own thing. I think then it comes down to your personal tastes, visual aesthetic, as a visual artist.

Newman: Often, game developers are at the mercy of their publishers for budget, major artistic and technical choices, and the marketing of the final project. When preparing a project for a client such as Linklater or Charles Schwab, what best practices do you recommend for keeping good communications and creating the desired product for the client?

Sabiston: Hm. It depends on the client, I guess. Some clients you work with closely and want to get as much of your own vision in there as well, because you truly care about the film, the subject matter, whatever. On the other hand, if your own ideas clash with theirs or they want to make all of the decisions, then they are the boss in my opinion. That's kind of what you have to accept with the money you get for working for someone else. I've learned on Schwab not to get too emotionally involved when your own artistic interests aren't at stake. It isn't worth the anguish if you don't get your way, and it is good practice I think to try to control your ego in that way, to really subscribe to the saying "The customer is always right." It can be annoying, though!

Newman: What advice do you have for young digital artists?

Sabiston: Really figure out just what it is that you enjoy, specifically, about the field you're in. And do that as much as you can. Part of getting out of school and going to work is the dreaded realization that no matter what you do, you are probably going to be stuck somewhere, doing something, for most of your days. If you can find something you enjoy enough to sit there and do it all day, every day, you are bound to get good at it.

9

CASTING

Casting a key piece of talent on a film project may be the thing that makes or breaks a movie production, but on a game production, this is rarely the case. Most game developers consider key game designers, engineers, or artists to be the talent that is highly desirable—and this is the talent that money is spent on. The only true casting that is done during the production of a video game usually centers around the voiceover work that will be done (recording the dialogue for the game's characters) and the actors that will be used during motion capture sessions.

New games, however, like UbiSoft's *Far Cry 2* have taken motion capture to the next stage by incorporating photorealistic action and movement to create an extremely lifelike cast of characters within the game. Motion capture has even been incorporated to record great detail on actors' faces to bring a new level of emotion and human reaction into a game.

Great motion capture techniques were used while producing UbiSoft's *Far Cry* series. Reproduced by permission of UbiSoft. All rights reserved.

Taking the time for proper casting can make a huge difference in the production value of a game. I've seen video game companies actually mine the production team for people to perform the voiceover work for characters within a game—this can usually be spotted pretty quickly when playing a game by the dialogue that is lackluster and emotionless. Imagine if a film production company approached a project in this manner! It would be unthinkable to cast a production assistant in a key voiceover role on a movie or send him or her in front of the camera without acting experience. Using experienced voiceover actors during production is a must for developing a true cinematic game and increases your production value immensely.

Thinking about possible candidates for casting can begin as early in development as preproduction. Although it would be helpful to have the voiceover script finalized before casting actors, it isn't necessary, as long as you know the gist of what each character will say and do, or what the individual characters' traits are (these can be recorded on character breakdown sheets). Just keep in mind (and let actors know) that games can take years to develop and you won't want to record the voiceover too early, as it may change.

9.1   Casting for Voiceover

Finding the right voice talent can be as simple as matching a voice to a character's face or hiring an experienced voice actor who can bring the level of emotion you want into the game. Either way, knowing how to deal with voice actors is key to getting the dialogue you want for the game. There are several things to focus on while casting/working with a voice actor:

1. *Match the qualities of an actor's voice with the qualities of the game character.* This means listening closely to how the actor speaks. Does he or she stutter? Is the actor easily excitable? Is there a predominant characteristic to the actor's voice? Remember that most actors can actually take direction (see Chapter 10, Directing), so give an actor the chance to produce the style of voice you want for your characters. As you will probably be casting for multiple roles within the game, it's best to do all the casting at once. That way, if an actor does not fit a specific role, you can allow him or her to read for other available characters within the game. Also, remember that actors can play multiple parts within a game.

2. *Make sure the actors can take direction.* If you followed the advice of the first guideline, this is the case. But, in case you haven't, run the actor through a series of different emotional types and levels—such as, "Let's try it with you being angry.

Okay, very angry. Now try reading this while barely control-ling your excitement." Getting an actor to perform in the manner you desire can take patience and a lot of explaining, so an actor who can respond to direction and understand what you want will save you time, money, and aggravation.

3. *Try to get experienced actors.* Although this is the most eas-ily disregarded guideline (especially if you have an ama-teur that perfectly fits a role), the more experienced an actor is, the easier you will get what you want in the least amount of time. Experienced actors are used to "cold read-ing" for auditions and are quick to adjust to changes in a script. These qualities help when recording in the studio with a limited amount of time and money. Trained actors also know how to take direction with little or no fuss.

4. *Pay attention to special casting needs.* Some roles require a specific kind of actor—especially comedy. Comedic timing is something only a small percentage of actors are good at. If you want the dialogue in the game to be convincing, you will need actors that can convince. Other special casting needs also include nontypical actors, such as old men/women, children, or individuals fluent in a foreign language.

Actor Michael Ironside is the voice of *Splinter Cell's* Sam Fisher. Reproduced by permission of UbiSoft. All rights reserved.

Also keep in mind that during casting calls, you do not have to make a decision right then and there. The best approach is to have one-page scripts (sometimes called "sides") of game dia-logue for several characters on hand and then have the actors read directly into a microphone. Record all of the sessions and then review the various voices once you're away from the actors before making any final decisions. Remember, you can always call back any actors that you think warrant further investigation, or if you think they would fit a role that they did not read for.

Because you are casting your actors just for their voice and style, it will only be necessary to record audio for voiceover casting sessions. When casting for motion capture work, however, the casting session will run a bit differently.

9.2   Casting for Motion Capture

The best approach for tackling a motion capture casting session is to think of it as casting for a silent movie. Pay attention to the body composition of the actors and how they match up with the game characters. You will want the actors' movements to be as close as possible to their game counterparts, so you will want them to have roughly the same build as the game character they are portraying. Sometimes called "performance capture" in the movie industry, motion capture is the process of capturing animation data from an actor who has been wired with equipment that monitors the actor's movements. This information is then used in conjunction with 3D modeling programs to create the finished character.

Though all games do not use this procedure, the advantages of using motion capture (mocap) are obvious. Information is gathered much quicker with the use of mocap, characters are digitized so that they can be seamlessly integrated into digital environments, and as you will not be using any practical effects (lighting, camera movement, and so on), you have the freedom to try out many different looks and strategies for the characters during production. Mocap is a unique technique and requires specific kinds of equipment, so you will probably do the work in a studio that specializes in this. However, you can do all the casting for the mocap work practically anywhere.

The newest *Resident Evil* game gets a lot of mileage out of top-notch character motion. Reproduced by permission of Capcom U.S.A., Inc. All rights reserved.

Before starting the casting session, make sure that the actors have access to the character breakdowns for the game. Character breakdown sheets basically describe the character and their role within the game. Knowing the specific characteristics of the characters before casting allows the actors to perform more accurately. For instance, if an actor is reading for a special operations commando, he or she will move with more agility, stealth, and precision, where an actor who is trying out for a clumsy sidekick might be a bit more awkward. Once actors understand who they are playing, run them through a series of movements. It's best to actually have a team member who has worked with motion capture on hand to help evaluate the actors (probably a lead artist and animator).

Remember, as you give the actor new motions to try, try to use the specific actions that the character will be performing within the game. Ideally, before the mocap casting session is even scheduled, a list of various movements should be detailed and made available for the auditions.

9.3   Using Celebrities

Adding a celebrity actor to the mix when recording voiceover can be a substantial plus when producing your game. Besides adding a new dimension of appeal to the gamer, experienced and known talent can bring a level of professionalism to the production that you would not have with an amateur on hand. Having a celebrity involved with production is also quite popular with the public relations/marketing department! Getting a celebrity can be as easy as contacting the actor's agent, but be aware of the possible negative aspects that are involved with dealing with "name talent".

Because an actor is a recognizable name in most households does not mean that they are experienced with voiceover work. This is doubly challenging when the actor does not like to take direction. Big-time celebrities typically do not like being told how to perform. Make sure that any celebrity you cast for the production will be fine with working with a team and taking cues from you. Another thing to keep in mind when casting celebrities is the big price tag that usually accompanies them. The later games in the *Wing Commander* series featured filmed cut-scenes with actors like Mark Hamill, Malcolm McDowell, and John Rhys-Davies—and the cost associated with these actors exceeded the budget for the programming team!

Finally, as you will be using the actor's name to an extent with selling your game, mete out the details regarding localizing that

Production Tip

 IMDb.com hosts an online database of all actors and lists contact information for them. At http://www.imdb.com, get the information for the actor's manager or agent, then contact them to solicit that person for employment.

actor's voice into other languages. Will the actor want to do it? Sometimes, they will already have an actor in place for foreign versions of their dialogue, and they may carry a hefty price tag as well.

Though the character Master Chief of *Halo* fame does not have a celebrity voice, good casting ensured that he has a good voice. Copyright © Bungie LLC and/or its suppliers. All rights reserved.

9.4 Finding Talent

There are several different methods to use when trying to find talent—it may be in your best interest to consider more than just one if you are unsure of any specific actors that may fit your production. The most widely used methods for getting to actors involve hosting casting calls, hiring a casting director, and using online casting sites.

Setting up a casting call can be a tricky thing. How many people do you want to actually read for the parts? Going overboard with putting out the word (using newspapers, magazines, sites, and so on) can quickly turn your casting call into a "cattle call"—actors' slang for a casting call with hundreds of people reading for the same part. Getting through that many actors all reading the same lines can be tedious, take up a lot of your time, and create frustration with the actors who are auditioning (imagine waiting in a long line for hours to read for a couple minutes—and be at your best when you do it). Using a focused casting call in perhaps a couple trade magazines may be the best way to approach this type of casting. An even smarter approach is to use a local, experienced casting director.

Casting directors are individuals who specialize in knowing local talent for a specific area. They are versed in local talent agencies and usually already have a pool of talent in place that they can call upon for specific types of roles. You can find your local casting directors usually listed in your state's (or city's) film production manual. Once you contact a casting director and send him or her the character breakdown sheets for who you are casting, they will either submit you a list of possible candidates, or set up a casting call for you. The great thing about using a casting director is that he or she will be more experienced with targeting specific people for specific roles, is aware of where to find them, and will be able to suggest to you the best method for acquiring them for the game.

If your budget does not allow for the hiring of a casting director—or if you have an experienced team member who has worked with voiceover and motion capture in the past—you may want to think about using online casting services for any talent you need. There are several sites that have services in this regard and most of them have nationwide searches/talent pools, so be cognizant of where an actor is located before soliciting them.

Another consideration when casting is that many actors belong to the Screen Actors Guild (SAG) or the American Federation of Television and Radio Artists (AFTRA). These are unions that protect actors' rights. If you will be using SAG or AFTRA actors, you will have to adhere to the union's guidelines regarding pay, work hours, and credit. Though nonunion actors are typically cheaper, they are also harder to find. Using a union allows you to use that union's online databases for actors and casting directors, as well as get any help from the union rep regarding casting.

9.5   Sides and Character Breakdowns

As mentioned before, take sides and character breakdown sheets with you to any casting call that you host. The sides are basically one-page pieces of dialogue for each character that you can have the actors read during the audition. As there probably won't be moments within a game where there is an entire page of straight dialogue (I hope), you can list four or five separate bits of dialogue or lines. Try to get varied emotion in these; include one angry piece of dialogue, one happy, and so on, to test the actor for all aspects of voice work.

The character breakdown sheets are pages that include the demographic information for each character, as well as a description and back story (see the sample character breakdown sheet in the Extras section of this book). This information includes the character's name, age, gender, and race (if relevant). Have the sides and character breakdowns in the waiting area of the casting call location so that actors get a chance to go over lines and study the character before reading.

Developer Tip

Try signing up for a free membership at Elite Casting Network (http://www.elitecastingnetwork.com). In addition to hosting thousands of actors' profiles, actors can include voiceover samples on the site so that you can review them without ever contacting them! The site also includes listings for casting directors.

Military games like *Call of Duty 4: Modern Warfare* are great at providing a character's background. Reproduced by permission of Activision. All rights reserved.

9.6 Auditions

Setting up a formal audition for actors is pretty straightforward. Once you have lined up a location (if you don't have an area within the studio for this, you can usually rent a room at a library or local VFW/Armory for casting purposes) and you have your finished sides and character breakdown sheets, you can proceed to the auditions. You won't need a lot of space, because the actors are only speaking and not performing in any other manner. Typically, before an actor is invited to the call, you can have them submit a resume and sample (usually called a "reel") to you directly. This step will help you weed out some of the actors that are obviously not right for the job. The resulting group is actually invited to the casting call.

On the day of the auditions, you will need someone to help with organizing and corralling the actors, someone to operate the recording device, and everyone who will be determining the final casting selections (including the casting director, if you are using one). Allow fifteen minutes for each actor to audition. This gives you time to talk with the actor for a bit to put him or her at ease and then allows for a couple different takes for each line of dialogue that is read.

Once the actors have read the lines, try giving them direction and see how they do. When they are finished, thank them and send them on their way. Make sure that each actor's recording is tagged and catalogued appropriately. Once you have chugged your way through all of the actors, you can then pack up and head back to the studio to review and judge the possible candidates for each character. If necessary, you can schedule "callbacks" to bring back

Developer Tip

As you will be taking a lunch break during the audition day, it's best to schedule auditions for two sessions: a morning session and an afternoon session. If you bring everyone out in the morning, when you go to lunch, actors will be standing around doing nothing for an hour or more—this tends to disgruntle everyone involved.

any actors you would like to hear again. Callbacks can also be great if somebody was really good, but you did not have a specific character for them at the time of the audition and do now.

When reviewing the audio recordings with the creative team, there are some key things you should pay attention to. How well did the actor enunciate the words? Was the speech clear or muddy? What about breathing? Was the actor able to speak with a nice pace, or were there gasps for air? Also note any accents, odd pitches, or rhythmic styles that an actor may have. These notes help with your final choices.

Although it may be tempting to do all of your casting by listening to demo reels submitted by actors, I advise against this. Having the actor actually audition allows you to see the actors in action, observe how he or she takes direction, and get an idea of how easy or hard it will be to work with the actor in the studio. Also, any way you cut it, using real people—real actors—to portray your game's characters is always be better and more cinematic than standard animation and inexperienced mocap actors.

Interview: Donise Hardy, Casting Director

Donise L. Hardy, CSA, began her casting career in San Francisco. After three years in that market, she then established her company in Los Angeles for six years, prior to moving to Austin, where she enjoyed eight years of working in the Texas market. Donise has cast hundreds of commercials, dozens of films (including *Cake* and *Jumping Off Bridges*) and industrials during her sixteen-year career and was one of the busiest casting directors in the state. She has also worked for the television programs *The Apprentice*, *The Jamie Kennedy Experiment*, and *America's Most Wanted*. Donise currently works and resides in Austin, TX.

Newman: What are the necessary steps to set up a quality casting call?

Hardy: There are several considerations. First the CD [casting director] has to get as much information pertaining to the job and talent as possible from the client in order to pass along a breakdown to agents that is precise, correct, and complete. Setting up the schedule is important in order to allow just enough time for the actor to perform, but not so much as to waste time throughout the day. Working closely with the agents in order to confirm or cancel appointments prior to the audition is imperative.

Newman: How do you ensure that you cast actors who are consistent with the style of the project and creative personnel involved?

Hardy: Dependent on the type of project (TV, film, commercial, VO [voiceover]), I rely heavily on the creatives to guide me. I try to always speak with the director to get his or her insight on what he or she "sees". I am also not reluctant to add my own vision to the project and usually bring in a few people who are not quite "right", just so the creatives have some interesting choices. And it is amazing how often they end up going with someone who didn't fit the specs!

Newman: When casting for voiceover work, how do you narrow the competition down a bit?
Hardy: The CD has to listen to a lot of demo tapes prior to the audition so as to not bring in a lot of people whose voices do not match the criteria.

Newman: Where do you find good voiceover talent?
Hardy: I use agents, especially those who specialize in VO talent. I rarely bring in a nonexperienced VO talent just because I like his or her voice. I want a professional when it comes to VO.

Newman: Though actors in animated sequences do not have to "act," per se, explain the process of matching an actor with a digital character.
Hardy: They have to act with their voices! This is very subjective casting and usually it boils down to the director hearing exactly what that character would sound like.

Newman: Do you usually cast "backups" for roles, or is it the norm to cast any replacements for a project on the fly?
Hardy: Many times clients will indicate a first, second, and sometimes third choice. They almost always get their first choice, but occasionally we do have to resort to a backup. We just keep our fingers crossed that the backup is still available. CDs normally will put backups on a "check avail" or "hold" *but* has to remember to release them twenty-four hours prior to the shoot or someone is going to pay them!

Newman: What types of information should a casting director ask for from voice actors? What are the advantages to using experienced voiceover actors?
Hardy: CDs don't usually ask many questions from VO actors. The actor has a demo reel and a resume to answer our questions. The advantage in using an experienced VO actor is that you know they are familiar with the equipment, the terminology, and the ability to make changes when directed to do so. The more professional the actor, the less time in the studio. In the long run, it usually costs the production company less money to hire a talent who is more expensive but can get it "in the can" faster, rather than paying the talent less money and having to book additional studio time.

10

DIRECTING

Though there are already directors in the world of game development—specifically, the creative directors and technical directors—when I use the word "director", I'm speaking of a person who actually works with actors. Dealing with actors during the motion capture process and while recording voiceovers are the primary areas we can address when discussing directing during game production, but there are several other areas that can be influenced by the use of solid techniques used by film directors. These include: directing concept meetings, location scouting, creating a unique vision with the cinematographer and/or engineering department, and making sure that all aspects of production are in sync with the script.

There is another kind of director in the game world as well—the person who actually directs the cut-scenes within a game, though this person is usually called a producer. As these cut-scenes usually double as at least part of the game's trailer and is the first asset to be used in the game's public relations campaign, this can be an important job during production. This type of producer is very similar to people in the film world that direct animated movies, so I will discuss this role as well.

When a new director is brought on board to direct a film, the first thing he or she does is take a look at the script and then organize and conduct a series of concept meetings.

10.1 The Concept Meeting

A "concept meeting" is the first time a film director meets the key participants from each department on a film shoot. There will be many meetings similar to this during preproduction of your game, but the most important thing to take away from a film's concept meeting is the use of department prioritizing. Besides making the artistic decisions regarding each area of production (for a film, this would be wardrobe, locations, props, and so on), there is a process of prioritizing the elements that are the most important and must come in under the budget and schedule first. This concept is equally important in game development; while in preproduction, it is important to implement the idea of the concept meeting to prioritize the features and levels that most clearly make the game unique and to get those into the game under the current budget and schedule. After these tasks have been identified, you will have a clear, prioritized list of assets that the coders and artists will have to begin production with.

With a clear cut story already in place, concepts for games like *Tom Clancy's Rainbow Six* series become much clearer. Reproduced by permission of UbiSoft. All rights reserved.

Another key point to conducting concept meetings is to get input from the heads/leads of each department—a system not unlike scrum, but more condensed and of longer duration. If you have properly developed a script for the game and it was distributed throughout the development team, everyone will have their own input as to what certain aspects of the game should look like and play like. Listen to them. One of the major advantages that the film industry has over the game industry is the ease of collaboration that exists in production. Nobody can make a film by themselves. This is true of games as well, so use it to the production's advantage.

Listen to the suggestions and ideas that each lead/department has and decide if they have merit. By incorporating their suggestions, you are fostering a sense of team building and you will not alienate any of the folks working on the game. Most of the time, discussions regarding artistic choices will be about the particulars of the game—but sometimes, the issue is more about control. When you hire experienced professionals to work on a game, sometimes they feel that their opinion is worth more than everyone else's. Be diplomatic about the issue, but nip this behavior in the bud immediately. Maintain your sense of vision and make sure that everyone on board is in sync with you.

10.2 Communicating Vision

Learning how to keep the team on the same page as a creative or technical director is a full-time job. It involves meetings, preparation, and communication. As discussed in earlier chapters, there are several tools at your disposal for keeping the original concept of the game in place as production proceeds. There are the aforementioned wiki pages, scrum, full blown meetings, emails, and so on. But how about command central?

Several prominent film directors are well known for keeping a sort of "motivational area" in the production offices. This is a place where the original concept art resides, character boards dot the walls, and even props/environmental pieces are kept. All of this effort is done to provide a place where artistic meetings can be held to make sure that everyone understands the central themes and look of the film being produced. This type of approach can also be taken at game studios. I have actually seen development teams put up concept art around the studio—but never to the extent that there is an actual meeting room where the creative and technical leads can go host a meeting and literally be surrounded by the atmosphere of the game.

An example of character concept art from the game *Tom Clancy's Ghost Recon Advanced Warfighter 2* by UbiSoft. Reproduced by permission of UbiSoft. All rights reserved.

Illustration by Jeff McFadyen
© Red Storm Entertainment, Inc.

At any rate, communicating on a daily basis with the leads about the logistics of the game is a must. Just make sure that in addition to the daily delta reports and tracking the status of the next milestone, you are constantly touching base to make sure that all the artistic decisions made regarding the game are still in place and that all the team is working with the same goals and vision—just don't get into the realm of meeting overload!

10.3   Location Scouting

Decisions regarding the locations used in a film ultimately come down to the director. A good director will choose locations that fit the needs of the budget but reflect the greatest amount of production value. A good location will also mirror the script as much as possible, so that on-the-spot changes will not have to be made during production. Locations in a video game on the other hand are usually a reference tool for the artists and designers so that they have a sort of road map when creating levels. Don't underestimate the importance of this, though!

Producers of Midway's *Blacksite: Area 51* actually went on location to Rachel, Nevada during preproduction of the game. Reproduced by permission of Midway Games. All rights reserved.

Lines of description in a script are often very succinct and contain only the barest amounts of information. An example: "Exterior Mountains, Winter." What kind of mountains? Are they snowcaps and really high? Are they low and flat? Are they in a heavily wooded area or maybe flatlands? The obscure language can make for conflicts in the art department and get early concepts off to a bad start. By scouting actual locations and taking pictures of the areas that illustrate levels in the game, you are providing materials for the production team to work from. You are also introducing a level of photorealism to the game; some people may think "cartoonish" when thinking of how an environment looks within a game—by showing them actual photos, they may take a more realistic and cinematic approach to designing the environments.

Working with actual locations is especially important when depicting real places in a game. Though you may alter the interiors of places to suit the levels of the game, keeping environments as realistic as possible will foster a level of immersion that created locales cannot match. Even fantasy games can use the information gathered at location scouts to create more realistic and cinematic environments. It is also important to use locations that have versatility. The more levels you can create from a single location, the better. This helps the schedule and therefore the budget.

The best approach is to take all the locations listed in the script (these will be extracted during the script breakdown process), prioritize them, and then brainstorm to see whether there are locales that can accommodate several different levels. For instance, one level might take place in a forest and another may take place in a research center. By choosing an observation station in the middle of Ozarks as your location, you kill two birds with one stone.

If your budget is such that flying to exotic locations is out of the question, don't forget about using books that feature detailed photographs of almost any site in the world. Your game doesn't have to suffer for lack of the scout.

Great locations contribute to the awesome *Ghost Recon Advanced Warfighter* game series. Reproduced by permission of UbiSoft. All rights reserved.

10.4   Working with the Cinematographer

Because games do not have a cinematographer on the production team, the typical form of collaboration that exists between a film director and film cinematographer will be less obvious. The camera angles, framing, and other such aspects of a game are all controlled by those who are creating the code, so it is essential to develop a strong rapport with the lead of that department regarding the artistic choices of the game. Game cinematography has come a long way and the more experienced game engineers now have a strong grasp of the basics of cinematography; if your lead does not, I suggest reading *Real-Time Cinematography for Games* by Brian Hawkins (Charles River Media, 2005).

Because there is an entire chapter (chapter 7) devoted to game cinematography, I will not belabor it here. Just remember that choices made regarding cinematography should be made by the game's producer or creative director, as they would be made by a film's director. It is the job of the game's programmers to get the cinematography up to par, but it is your job to direct them.

10.5   Directing Talent

Once the actors have been cast for the voiceover work (and for the motion capture), they must be directed during the recording sessions. There are several steps that you can take to make sure that you get the best possible takes during the session. First, you will want to make sure that the actors have gotten the script as early as possible. This step gives them time to memorize their lines and get comfortable with speaking the lines (especially if there are any technical or difficult phrases in the dialogue). You can also ensure the actors are on the same page as you with direction by annotating the script with any notes that are important, such as indicating when a line is yelled or when a particular piece of dialogue is tinged with a particular emotion.

When the actors have arrived at the studio to record, sit down with them and make them comfortable. As they have had time with the script to learn the dialogue, they will usually be put at ease with a simple conversation. Once everyone is acquainted and the studio is ready to proceed, move into the recording area. The various lines that must be recorded should be listed on the script and annotated with the information that you will use to store the data for incorporation into the game. Begin with the first line, and once you are happy with the recorded piece of dialogue, move on to the next.

Hopefully, there will be no major snags with getting what you need from the actors, but if you do remember to be tactful and to carefully explain the context of the spoken line to the actor and the desired emotion you want—just know that actors can be sensitive to "line reading" exactly by the numbers. When you hire an actor, you are also hiring their personality, so expect it to be injected into the dialogue. Usually, most conflicts arise from confusion. Clarify the scene and what you want and most situations are quickly remedied.

Capcom's *Lost Planet: Extreme Condition* features well-executed dialogue. Reproduced by permission of Capcom U.S.A., Inc. All rights reserved.

Working with motion capture also has the added logistics of attaching motion capture equipment to the actor (so allow for more time with the actor at the studio) and blocking off the movements that will be recorded during the session. Just as you did with the voiceover actors, make sure to send the actor a list of all the shots you want as soon as possible so that he or she can rehearse (it may even be a good idea to rehearse and direct the actor prior to the actual date of recording to make sure that he or she knows what will be required). As movements may be limited by the capture equipment, make sure that each action is done succinctly. It's also a good idea to record the session with a video camera. If the session goes well, you can have the recording to use for future productions (you can also use a bad session as a "lesson learned" during the postmortem of the game.

10.6   Script Supervision and Continuity

On a film set, there is a person called the "script supervisor". This person is responsible for making sure that continuity is in place and that all the various scenes that are being shot are being done so with a singular look or style. A script supervisor is also responsible for making sure that every prop ends up where it is supposed to be when moving on to the next scene (sometimes a very tedious job). Continuity within a game is a big issue as well. This task should be approached from the artistic and creative slants and implemented from the very beginning.

Creative continuity is as simple as making sure that all assets are accessible to the entire team. When an artist or animator is working on a new character, he or she will want to make sure that it is in sync with all of the game's other assets. The easier this is to accomplish, the more continuity and consistent style you will have within your game. It can also mean voicing opinions during scrum regarding certain elements that do not feel right or seem to match up with the rest of the game. Encourage individual team members to inform the leads when this is the case. And listen to them! Because they are working on the small details of every asset within the game, they are much more intimately familiar with them. If minor changes need to be made to a look, environment, or even the script, then do it. Use this collaboration to produce the best possible game.

On the technical front, good continuity is something that you may want to ask the quality assurance department to be particularly vigilant with. How many times have you played a game—an FPS, for example—where the enemy was killed using a technique on one level, but on the next level it simply did not work at all. Why? Nothing changed, so what happened? Bad continuity. Keeping consistency throughout the game will help with immersion, keep frustration levels down (and therefore the fun levels up), and simply make the world you have created seem more real.

10.7   Directing Cut-Scenes

More and more, it is becoming the norm to have producers that are specifically skilled at creating cut-scenes and game trailers. Although for immersion's sake, it's best to keep the cut-scenes at a minimum—or at least keep them extremely short—there are usually at least two in a game. The "mandatory" two cut-scenes you'll find within a game will be one at the very beginning of the game to introduce the story and one at the very end of the game when you've "beaten" the main story line. Arcade-style games may contain no cut-scenes at all, but instead show an animation on the menu screen. Either way, the cut-scenes designed for the game usually double for at least part of the game's trailer.

Because a game trailer (and an in-game cut-scene) is a sort of mini animated movie, you can use a scaled-down version of the production process to create them. In other words, because you know the story of the entire game, create a small script of the story pieces that will be used within the trailer, storyboard them, then create the art/ environments and develop the scenes. It would be wise to take a long look at the cut-scenes that will already be within the game play and then take as much as possible from them for the trailer. This approach keeps the costs and time constraints down for creating trailers.

Of all the producers in the game industry, producers who specialize in cut-scenes and trailers are the most film-like and usually have the highest population of individuals who have been educated at a film school. As cut-scenes/trailers are not interactive, it is necessary to make sure that the tone and style of the game are evident to gamers who watch them. Another concern will be the marketing department. Before writing the script for the game trailers, consult the marketing department to see what features or elements will be the focus for selling the game and include those elements in the trailers. This step will make the PR folks very happy. It will also take some of the heat off you if anyone dislikes the trailers.

Again, script it out and storyboard it first though. This lets the creative director and producers take a look at what you're going to do and make any changes or suggestions.

10.8   Cut-Scenes Versus In-Game Cinematics

As mentioned prevously, a game ideally has as few cut-scenes as possible. If you were told that for every minute of time you force a gamer to watch a cut-scene it takes that same gamer about thirty minutes to get fully immersed into the game again, you would keep the amount and duration of cut-scenes at a minimum, wouldn't you? Well, for some gamers, this is exactly the case. It's understood that a short cut-scene should give you an idea of what's going on at the beginning of the game and that an ending will be provided for you to get that last bit of satisfaction from conquering the game. But to force gamers to constantly watch extended cut-scenes for game information is simply a crime. It's not a good cinematic experience and it's not fun interactivity. It's frustrating. And, of course, the absolute worst crime to commit is to provide no way for the gamer to press a button and skip the cut-scenes! If a particular level is hard, and a gamer must make many attempts at beating it, watching a mandatory cut-scene creates huge frustration and anger.

Ubisoft does a great job of integrating first-person perspective cut-scenes in the game *Far Cry Instincts: Predator.* Reproduced by permission of UbiSoft. All rights reserved.

If you must provide information within the game, do it during the game play as much as possible. What if a movie paused the action and took you to a text-only screen to let you read about the background of the next scene? Would the movie be made better by the addition of more information, or would you lose all suspension of reality and become disinterested? Some games, like Ubisoft's *Far Cry Instincts: Predator,* have done a great job of keeping all dialogue and info in a first-person format within the game.

One of the biggest things you will hear in game circles when discussing making a game cinematic is that most producers think of a cinematic game as having more cut-scenes and more dialogue within the game. This is exactly wrong. A cinematic game is immersive, real, and fosters the suspension of reality, which means fewer cut-scenes and less dialogue.

Interview: Jay Duplass, Director

Jay Duplass was born in New Orleans and studied film at the University of Texas in Austin. In 2002 Jay collaborated with his brother Mark on *This Is John*, a short film shot digitally for $3 dollars. It was accepted into Sundance (2003) and earned the brothers a representation deal with William Morris. They returned to Sundance in 2004 with another digitally shot short, *Scrabble*. The following year, they premiered their third short, *The Intervention*, at Berlin (2005), where it won the Silver Bear and the Teddy Award. 2005 also marked the release of Jay and Mark's feature film debut, *The Puffy Chair*, which premiered at Sundance (2005), won an audience award at SXSW (2005), and was a part of the "best of the fest" at Edinburgh (2005). Jay recently finished work on the Duplass Brothers' second feature, *Baghead*, and is now working on his third feature film, *The Do-Deca-Pentathlon*.

Newman: There has been a strong convergence between the film and game industries in the last few years. What elements do you see in video games that remind you of movies? What characteristics draw you, as a film director, to a video game?

Duplass: Well, to be honest. I don't really play video games, 'cause I'm afraid I'll get addicted and then I won't get anything done. My brother Mark, however, is addicted to *BrickBreaker* on his phone, and had to go cold turkey during the shooting of our last film.

Newman: You are credited as cinematographer on your last film, *Baghead*. What is your process regarding directing the camera, or at least knowing the specific type of framing or shot you want in a scene?

Duplass: My process is to not plan things out and to let the actors do their thing and to capture it as it happens. In terms of framing, I definitely have axis and look space, and so on in the back of my mind, but mainly I just try to not think, and just shoot what I want to see.

Newman: You are also credited as the screenwriter for your last two features (*The Puffy Chair* and *Baghead*)—do you find it hard to adapt the work of an outside screenwriter or author to the screen? How would you describe the artistic process of interpreting words to images?

Duplass: I don't really think of it as adapting words to screen. I think of the screenplay as a template and a starting point to get things rolling. Then when we get onto set, I try to just foster whatever the actors are bringing that day, make sure it works in the whole scheme of the movie, and just get the most natural and interesting stuff I can get.

Newman: When you're coming up with characters for your films, to what extent do you actually develop them? Do you have pretty detailed character breakdowns for your movies?

Duplass: We mostly base our characters on people we've known. So we don't really create them out of nowhere. We don't do breakdowns unless we have to. We mostly just talk with our actors about them and tell them all the funny and wonderful and horrible things about them and try to get them inspired about who that person is. But more than that, it's about finding out what the actor is inspired by, and then going down that path.

Newman: Being an independent film producer, I'm sure you're always looking for ways to keep your budget down when shooting a feature film—such as avoiding exotic locations. In your opinion, what kind of impact does your choice of locations have on the cinematic value of your movies?

Duplass: Well, our movies are really about domestic situations on some level—situations that most of us would find ourselves in—so we're a bit lucky in that we don't feel like we need exotic locations … yet.

Newman: Another aspect of shooting independent films involves the use of "noncelebrity" actors—a concern for most independent video games as well. Describe your approach or method for casting key characters in your movies.

Duplass: Our characters are based on people we love, and think are hilarious. In terms of casting for that, it's all about actors we love and are inspired by. We put them together and try to make it feel real … try to find life in there. In auditions, we see things, and it either opens doors and excites us or not.

Newman: What about directing actors with little or no experience? Is there an approach that has worked well for you on the set?

Duplass: The main thing I tell nonactors is not to try. There's nothing they have to do except be there and be themselves. It's my job to elicit anything that I want. So they don't have to worry. It's all about disobligating them in a way. I tell them that they've done all they need to do just by being there, and the rest is up to me. In that way, you eliminate any "acting", the behavior is real, and then you can just try to add things as you go. But the most important thing for our movies is that the underlying behavior is realistic and genuine.

Newman: Do you think the game industry has affected the film industry in its approach to style or content? What about the influence of film upon the game industry?

Duplass: Absolutely, they both affect each other. It seems that gaming has become more narrative.

Newman: In your position, I'm sure you are approached quite often with scripts, ideas, and books for possible future films. How do you determine whether what you are reading (even when it's your own work) will translate into a great film? What elements do you look for in pitches and proposals that indicate a great project?

Duplass: To be honest, we really don't read that much. We spent one year reading hundreds of scripts our agent sends, and realized that the odds of us finding something that fits us more than something we'd write for ourselves is extremely low. So the time is just not worth it. That being said, this sounds simple and corny, but you just know when it's right to do something. It's all about instinct and trusting your gut. And more specifically than that, we always are asking ourselves, are we the best people in the world to make this particular film. If not, we turn it down.

11

SOUND DESIGN

Films and games are both thought of as a visual medium, but the reality is that sound plays almost as important a part in the final product. In addition to tackling every piece of music within a game, a sound designer/engineer must also track down (and usually must record) every sound effect, piece of dialogue, and ambient sound within the game (this includes wind, water, city street, and so on). These are pretty much the same assets for which a sound designer would be responsible when making a movie. Because of this, many sound designers have worked in both areas, games and movies, as well as applying their trade to theatre productions and television.

Excluding the music, the sounds that you will import into the game will either be a sound effect (like an explosion or a space-ship taking off), a practical sound (car door shutting or footsteps), or ambient/room tone (crowd in a mall, applause, or wind

In addition to the killer artistic choices made on the game *Saboteur* by Pandemic, sound will play an important part in the game's success. Reproduced by permission of Pandemic Studios. All rights reserved.

blowing through the trees). Each of these types of sound has its own set of challenges in obtaining them.

Becoming an effective sound designer means having a great ear for hearing what the best possible sounds are for a specific project—as well as knowing how to find and obtain those sounds. There are many sources for these sounds—all of which will be discussed later in this chapter—but the key for success as a sound designer lies in matching an audio style with the visual theme of the project; this can be as simple as importing authentic sounds and music for a game set in the 1930s, or as difficult as creating all the sounds for a possible future within a sci-fi game. Sound design includes every sound within the game down to the basics—the most basic of all sounds within a game and film comes from the soundtrack and background music.

11.1   Cinematic Music

Most of the time, sound designers work with the creative heads of a production to come to an agreement as to what type/genre of music fits the project best. In some cases, this decision has already been made by the game's creative director and this choice has led to a particular sound designer. Though some designers work in all genres of music and styles, most specialize in a particular area—usually because most sound designers are musicians and play in a certain style. Some designers also segue into the field of sound design because of experience working as a sound engineer in a studio or have worked as a sound editor for a film. Either way, if the designer has the ability to compose and perform a certain type of music, this is an easy way to lower your budget in that department a bit—it means not contracting out to a composer or performer for your game's music (or at least a portion of it).

If you have chosen a designer that does not compose music, or does not work in the style of music you want for the game, the sound designer will shop around for a composer or performer who is already writing in the style desired and is close to the expectations of the creative director. Music is one of the easiest ways to create a uniform tone within a game, so it is important that decisions made in regard to musical choices be done very carefully. Some of the things to consider when working with music are:

- What genre or style of music do you want?
- What is the music trying to do?
- How many different pieces of music do you need?

When working on a budget, hiring a sound designer who is skilled in creating electronic (or loop-based) music is a great choice. Most of these programs can be bought for very little cash and learning how to manipulate and create loops can be learned quickly. Also, most modern sound designers are accustomed to working on a computer for mixing and editing, so it is no great leap to incorporate loops.

A great and inexpensive alternative to composing electronic music is to use unsigned bands for the game's music (if that type of music is going to fit the project). One trip to MySpace will educate you on the sheer amount of musicians working throughout the world. Pick ten or twenty bands that are playing the style of music you want to use and ask for permission to use one of their songs in your game—sometimes, you can even get an instrumental version of the songs from them, as most unsigned musicians retain the tracks from their recording sessions. Make sure you get a legal permissions form signed from them, though, before using the music in the game. Getting licensing from signed musicians/composers takes quite a bit of time, so if you're going to go this route, you may want to start this process as early as possible—probably in preproduction.

Once you have obtained the music for the game—with the guidance of the creative director—the sound designer can move on to working on the game's other audio needs. Before you can actually record, though, you probably need a few pieces of equipment and software.

11.2 Tools for Great Sound

Getting all the various audio assets for the game requires some specific equipment and software. Typically, most dialogue is

Production Tip

There are several different types of loop/music software. Download the free version of Sony's ACID Pro—ACID XPress—and give the program a try. Sony also sells CDs of royalty-free loops that you can use to create the music for your game.

Check out the original soundtrack for *Elder Scrolls IV: Oblivion* by Jeremy Soule for an example of great, original game music. The Elder Scrolls IV: Oblivion® © 2006 Bethesda Softworks LLC, a ZeniMax Media company. All rights reserved.

Production Tip

If you're using electronic music in your game, how would you like to have a musician like Moby supplying some of the tunes? Moby actually offers free or inexpensive use of many of his songs to independent filmmakers and game designers. You can apply for a one-time use license at his Web site: http://MobyGratis.com.

recorded in an actual studio with the sound designer present—or at least a competent engineer who supervises the session and submits the recordings for approval. Sound effects and great ambient/room/environmental sounds must be obtained in the field. To accomplish this, you need a field recorder (probably one that records to digital audio tape) or sampler with a studio-quality microphone and headphones.

The equipment for recording can be quite expensive—chances are good that you will do your voiceover work in an external sound studio—so finding a sound designer who already owns his or her own gear for field recording is another way to trim the budget. Make this a consideration during hiring. The software, on the other hand, will have to be licensed by your production company, so you must make some careful decisions regarding these choices.

Most of the required software is computer-based recording programs, and there are quite a few of these on the market, so try them out before buying. You should consult with the sound designer as well to see if he or she has a preference or any experience working with a particular program. Some of the more prevalent programs include Pro Tools, Cakewalk Sonar, and Sony Soundforge. You also need an interface to connect the recorder to your computer to upload the sound files. Again, this is a common piece of equipment, so the sound designer may already own one.

The final consideration (though probably the first tackled) is how all the sounds will be imported into the game. For this, consult with the technical director or lead to determine the best audio format, compression, and so on for getting everything into the game. This may require the purchase of another piece of software (usually called "audio middleware") and may be a factor when choosing the game's engine. All of these choices should be made in preproduction along with the creative decisions regarding audio.

11.3   Sound Effects and Sampling

There are several different ways to get all the audio assets you need for your game that have been used in the film industry for years—these include contracting out to independent audio/sound personnel, buying prepackaged sound effects, and recording your own sounds in the field. Contracting out should be considered only if the sounds needed are unavailable otherwise, as that is the most costly method of obtaining what you need.

Development Tip

For more details and tutorials on sound design, visit http://filmsound.org. It provides a wealth of information and history about film, television, and game sound design. You can also get tips on how to find and record specific effects at http://epicsound.com and at http://game-sound.org.

Getting great sound effects for war-based games like *Tom Clancy's Rainbow Six: Vegas 2* can be quite a challenge. Reproduced by permission of UbiSoft. All rights reserved.

Prepackaged sound effects are available from many companies. You can usually download the files directly from the companies' sites (just be sure to sample them first and make sure that they are of a high enough quality to use in the game) or purchase CDs of common sounds. These CDs are sold with names like "Sounds of the Jungle" or "Military and Weapon Sounds". These types of sound effects can save you a lot of leg work when trying to record everything you need in the field. Once you have obtained everything you can using this cost-effective method, you can then tackle getting all the miscellaneous stuff you'll have to record on site.

Going out on location to record means taking a small sound team, a recorder or sampler, and a microphone/headset to the actual locales where the sounds can be obtained. You may have to do this because the particular sound you want is nowhere to be found otherwise, or it may be a very specialized sound (say, rocks bouncing off a piece of plastic then hitting water) that simply has not been archived anywhere. Either way, going out to get the sounds is an inevitable task during development.

Once you get to the site, set up for recording the sound by making sure that you can duplicate the sound you need multiple times—though this may seem obvious, some sounds are difficult to obtain and getting one take is usually not enough. When this is done, you can then attach the headset and microphone to the recorder. One person should point the microphone as close as possible to the sound (make sure that this is a unidirectional microphone, like a shotgun mic, so that you will pick up the least amount of external noise as possible—unless of course you are shooting ambient or environmental sound, which would require a good omnidirectional microphone) while the other person monitors the recorder through the headset to make sure that the signal is strong and clear with no interference or outside noise.

Games like UbiSoft's *Tom Clancy's Ghost Recon Advanced Warfighter 2* contain hundreds of practical sounds. Reproduced by permission of UbiSoft. All rights reserved.

Once you have obtained the sound you want, you can then remove the media (usually a digital audio tape or digital media card) and label it for download later at the studio. This is pretty much the process you will use to get everything on location. Before heading out, though, here are some questions you should consider:

1. How many different environments/locations are sounds needed from?
2. How many individual sounds will you need from each location?
3. How much space (media/tapes) do you need to capture several takes of each sound?

The logistics involved in good sound design is yet another aspect that should be discussed while making the game's schedule and budget. Having the sound engineer or designer present when doing the script breakdown is another way to tally up the sounds and sound locations during preproduction.

11.4 Effective Sound Design

Remember that as you develop and obtain all the audio assets you need for your game, the sound design for a game is an ongoing process. As the art department and engineers develop assets for the game, they turn to the sound designer to bring them to life. Thus the total number of sound effects and sounds for the game will be constantly increasing. It is important then to make sure that the sound designer understands how the other departments work and how they document assets that are being produced. Major locations will be identified early in the development cycle (hopefully during preproduction, in a script), so getting ambient sounds and general effects from those places can be done early, but the other thousand individual sounds that inevitably pop up must be gotten during the production cycle.

Effective sound design, like in the newest *Ace Combat* game, makes a great game. ACE COMBAT® 6: FIRES OF LIBERATION ™ © 2007 NAMCO BANDAI Games Inc. All trademarks and copyrights associated with the manufacturers, aircraft, models, trade names, brands, and visual images depicted in this game are the property of their respective owners, and used with such permissions. Courtesy of NAMCO BANDAI Games America Inc.

Treat the sound department just as you would any other in the production team and allow them to contribute to the wiki pages, do daily delta reports, and otherwise participate. Keeping the sound department integrated with development makes your production team run much smoother, keeps the sound design on point, and gets you the most effective and cinematic game possible.

Interview: Marc Schaefgen, Sound Designer

Newman: Sound is such a huge part of the cinematic experience. How do you approach working on a new project?

Schaefgen: With games, we have a unique situation in that we do not really get a postproduction phase. You are constantly chasing the tail of change during what would normally be a postproduction period. Some games have done it successfully, but it takes mad production skills and a team that can consistently hit deadlines, which is a rare combination. So, with that knowledge, you have to create a process that fits with the game style and the team dynamic. Each game process might be slightly different, but

I generally approach them all from the same high-level mindset. Developers have many ways to slice the development pie, but most agree that game development has three very distinct phases: concept, prototype, and production. Audio should really be no different than any other part of the production and align their goals with the rest of the team. For the concept phase, those main goals should be to outline the game play and its systems, and to set the tone and vision. During the prototype phase, you are proving out those game play concepts while also demonstrating your ability to deliver on the overall vision or experience.

During the concept phase for audio, I like to create three main documents: the music, SFX [sound effects], and voice style guides. From those three main documents, subdocuments are created that help to further define those styles; each style requires a different approach to its documentation. For instance, from the music style guide, I create a music reference compendium. This compendium is composed of music samples taken from all types of media (TV, games, film), that to me expresses the emotion, style, and instrumentation that is indicative of what I want the final score to be like. The important partner to this compendium is the reference guide that goes into detail about each music sample, why it was chosen, likes and dislikes, instrumentation notes, and any other pertinent information that I feel is appropriate. Do not be shy at this point. Spelling out your vision clearly to everyone involved is critical to moving forward and finalizing schedules and budgets. That is just the music angle to the project. For sound design and voice, I go down similar but different paths, defining the style. When it comes to voice, the writing plays a major factor in the vocal style, thus demonstrating the need for collaboration with the team leaders during every phase of development.

The prototype phase is akin to what film calls preproduction. In film, for the most part, your technology is standardized. You use the same cameras, software programs, compositing tools, and so on as the next guy. In games, not so much. Your technology is your mojo. Even developers that license their development technologies enhance and combine those technologies in ways that no other developer would. So this is the time to prove to the people that write the checks that your team has what it takes to make this product. You need to instill that confidence at all levels, and audio is no exception. By the end of the prototype phase (which can last more than a year, and sometimes multiple years) you should have what is commonly referred to as a "vertical slice". That is, a small excerpt or demo of your product that demonstrates every major facet of that product and proves that you can build the rest of the product to a reasonable schedule and budget.

Production phase is where all the real hard work comes. This is where audio is churning right alongside everyone else. There are no shoots, or dailies, or dubs needed for rough cuts. We build the audio for the game as the game itself is being built. This requires solid scheduling of resources and at times bulking up staff temporarily either in-house or off-site, to ensure that those schedules can be met.

Newman: When balancing music with dialogue, what types of considerations do you take to make sure you get the best possible mix?

Schaefgen: As games are nonlinear, you sometimes have no idea when a line of dialogue is going to play, and what other sound sources at that time are already playing. When I start a project, I determine one of two ways to approach this issue. The first is the easiest, which is to use a ducking mechanism, so that when any line or dialogue or a selected line of dialogue is played, all other sounds (or a selected set of sounds) are reduced in volume by a certain amount. This trick ensures that those lines of dialogue will be audible in the mix no matter what other sounds are present. Because this is done systemically, it is less time-consuming for the mixer to balance properly.

The second method, which is more difficult, but also my preferred method, is to create a mix where the dialogue is always going to be audible. This might entail periodic uses of ducking, but not in a systemic fashion. It requires an extensive amount of testing and tweaking, consistently playing the game, tweaking levels, playing the game, tweaking levels, until the production team makes you stop. This method isn't as efficient or fun, but the results are more compelling in my opinion. When you use ducking systemically, it has a tendency to be distracting and pull the user out of the immersion of the experience. I have used ducking to success in a situation where all dialogue was delivered by changing the screen to a letter-box format to evoke a cinematic vibe to the delivery. This change in visual made the change in audio acceptable.

Newman: Speaking of music, how do you determine the most appropriate style or genre of music to use to fit the mood of a project?

Schaefgen: This comes about during the concept phase and is largely a team effort. Game development is about working with a team. During the concept phase, the team is smaller and generally composed of the major decision makers of the project, which makes collaboration much easier. I am constantly talking to the game designers and artists about what their visions are and reading documents that they create to backup their visions, just like

I am doing with audio. I dissect, examine, reread, ask questions, call meetings—everything I can do to gain the most information about what everyone is converging on in terms of vision and style.

Armed with that knowledge, I look to my personal taste and how I would want the score to evolve. Then I also look at the competition; what my peers in this genre are doing stylistically. If I see developers taking chances, I might be inclined to be more risky with my score style. If I see them being conservative and complacent, do I follow suit, or really break the mold? It all depends on the combination of project style, genre style, trends, and what I think will help immerse the player in the game experience. It all comes down to that one thing though—what is best to enhance the game play experience—all else pales in importance.

From there, I dig up a small quantity of music samples that I think hit the overall style and tone. Then I play those for the music stakeholders on the team and we go from there. This can be a long process of listening and digging for tunes, and listening some more. Getting those stakeholders to sit in a room together and be silent to listen to their musical choices is very important to them signing off on the style. Once we all agree, I build the rest of the music reference compendium and send that out to the stakeholders for feedback. One more time I make them sit in a room, listen, and comment. This listening time not only engages the stakeholders, but gives me the ability to understand their wants and needs and how to best accommodate the project.

Newman: When working with any form of live music (orchestra, band, and so on), what are some of the factors that influence the quality of the score?

Schaefgen: Emotion, emotion, emotion. A machine cannot emote the way a human does. Also, not every musician is going to emote in exactly the same way. Having a singular violinist play many parts all multitracked together in a small studio room will never sound like a string section in a beautiful-sounding hall where each musician contributes their own style and emotion to the music. But then again, it all depends on your musical style. For *BlackSite: Area 51*, we chose to not use live players in order to put that budget toward a lengthier score. It worked well for that game, because stylistically electronic instruments were a big part of the sound palette. Were it a purely orchestral score, then having live players would have greatly enhanced the emotional delivery.

In games, it is a bit of a trade-off and is constantly looked at as an area where the budget can be trimmed. Luckily, the level of quality demanded by the consumer is constantly growing. In film, no big-budget title would consider not using an orchestra to record the organic parts of the score—it is too common and not even a consideration. In games, however, it is not the norm and therefore scrappy game designers and audio directors fight the battle for quality at every revision of the budget spreadsheet. Once the consumer demand is high enough, developers of big-budget games will have to use live orchestras to remain competitive.

Newman: A lot of the challenges involved with good sound design seem to originate with special effects. How do you tackle recording sound effects on a location?

Schaefgen: Gathering decent source material is always a challenge for sound designers, but it also one of the more fun parts of the job. Midway has a commercial sound library that totals more than 800 GB; our proprietary internal library is much smaller, less than 100 GB. We are constantly striving to find new unique sound sources for our products. We have field recording gear, portable recorders, microphones, and accessories that we use to gather unique sounds out in the world. We have had a lot of construction around our offices in the last two years, so we have taken advantage of that in our field recordings. We have done gunshot recordings, car recordings, recordings of sounds in the desert, the city streets—anywhere we can find appropriate material. My team has open ears and is always on the listen for new and unique sounds.

Newman: Listening to the audio track of the game *Blacksite: Area 51*, it becomes obvious that there are specific musical cues that set the tone for the action that follows. Explain the process of determining where these cues should occur and how to implement them.

Schaefgen: For *BlackSite*, we decided to use the character classes as a basis for creating the musical themes that would weave in and out and create the main score. Also, each character class had unique instrumentation that created the sonic signature in the score. There were three main classes: humans (more specifically, soldiers), aliens, and alien/human hybrids. Depending on the dominant races for a given game-play scenario, we used a mix of themes and instrumentation that would cover those classes. Because the game was fairly linear in nature, we generally knew what was coming next, based on geographic location, so we used triggers placed in the world to cue music. Music was also controlled based on game states or AI [artificial intelligence] states. We didn't want wall-to-wall music, so between encounters we opted for either no music or very low ambient cues.

Newman: The game and film industries both rely on the quality of audio immensely. What lessons have you have learned from the film industry that would help a new sound designer?

Schaefgen: A lot of game audio production is the same as film. We use Pro Tools and scads of plug-ins, we record our own source material, we work closely with the visionaries of the project to enhance that vision through sound, and so on. It didn't use to be that way. Before digital audio was the norm and processing power was plentiful, developers synthesized all of the sound content for a game. So our process of making games hasn't been influenced a whole lot by film, but the process for making the *content* that goes into the game has. Like I mentioned earlier, we don't really get a postproduction phase. The game development cycle is very different from that of a film production, but it is still media. Media that is digitized and manipulated to evoke some sort of response from the player.

In this day and age, I feel that film has a lot more to learn from games than the other way around. The game industry had been studying the film industry for so long that they thought they wanted to be just like film, but soon after, realized the differences are there for a reason and that games are a unique artform and a totally viable means of expression on their own.

Newman: What advice do you have regarding getting the best possible finished project?

Schaefgen: Assemble the strongest team possible and let those people do what they do best. Facilitation is more important than ego. Get out of the way and provide the support they need to be successful. Communication is the next most important factor. Once your team is empowered, they need to be efficient and informed. Establishing and maintaining strong lines of communication between all disciplines is the key to success. Everything after that is gravy.

Part 3

CREATING YOUR OWN CINEMATIC PROJECT

12

GETTING STARTED

Graduating from a university, community college, or tech-oriented school and moving straight into a game development job can be a daunting task…so hopefully you are one of the fortunate (and probably hard-working) members of this community who has stormed from the chute and landed a job developing a game at an established company. Besides saving you lots of money and headaches associated with creating your own game, a thriving game studio will already have the resources in place to develop, publish, and sell a successful title. However, if you are not one of these folks, do not despair! Getting your own game studio up and running can be as simple (or as hard) as creating your first game.

With game tools like Microsoft's XNA becoming widely available and affordable, it is not an unreasonable venture to get your first game out in the market without a huge investment of time or money. Chances are good that you probably started or maybe even finished a game while in school. Becoming an "independent" game developer (meaning that you do not have the backing of a publisher) means having complete control of your project. It also means accepting complete responsibility for any success or failure associated with the game! Being an indie studio also means something else; it suggests a philosophy of trying out new ideas and styles of game play that large developers would never attempt—mostly due to the lack of marketing numbers to support the type of concept you've created or that the game is simply not squarely centered in a current gaming trend.

Garnering success from an avant-garde game is great way to get noticed in the game industry and a quick way to get your game noticed. But how do you become an independent game developer?

Development Tip

Sign up for Microsoft's XNA Creator's Club (http://creators.xna.com). In addition to hosting forums to discuss issues with working with the program, users can demo other games being created, post their own game demo, and access resources for further education.

12.1   Setting Up Your Video Game Company

Though there are many logistics associated with creating a new company—such as whether to incorporate and getting your funding (both discussed later)—fundamentally, your new game company will be made or broken based upon one thing: your game. Making a wise decision about your first project will be the single biggest factor regarding the amount of success you will have as a developer (check out the interviews with Warren Spector, chapter 2, and Richard Rouse III in this chapter). Success as a studio, however, has several influential elements that must come together in order for you to survive in the game industry.

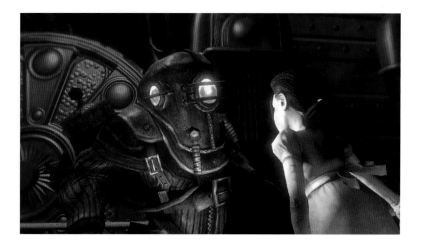

Successful game studios like Irrational become successful by making wise game decisions. Reproduced by permission of 2K Games. All rights reserved.

In addition to a great game concept, you need startup funds and the resources necessary to create your first game: hardware, software, and skilled talent. Depending on the scope of your game design, creating a new title can take anywhere from five to fifty people working full-time for many months to get the job finished. Each of these people needs a workstation and the tools to do their job. This means money. Lots of money. There are several ways to get the money and equipment you need—and chances are good that you will tackle all of these ways.

Before approaching a bank and trying to get any kind of small business loan, do your best to bring down the amount of money you need to borrow. With any luck, and with lots of resources on hand, you won't have to get a loan at all. The first thing you can do is to try and hire people who have their own equipment and software. This will be reasonably easy for artists, as they tend to work a lot from home anyway, and the popular programs used when creating digital art are widely available and reasonably priced. Depending on the programming language and/or game engine you use, though, programmers will present the greatest challenge in acquisition. Although getting programmers fluent in the programming language you are using may be relatively easy, getting a programmer familiar with a particular game engine or middleware can be a challenge.

As a producer, if you are able to get an entire team together whose members have the ability to work from home, you will essentially be functioning as a studio with an entire contractor/consultant-based workforce. Working this way saves you money, in that you don't actually need a physical studio or workplace for all the employees to work at (so no rent and no bills there) and you won't have to buy any computer equipment to populate it. It will also make your job easier when it comes to hiring talent. If you live in a nongame development center (like anywhere other than Austin, Texas or San Francisco, California), you would probably have a rather small pool of local talent to draw your employees from. By doing everything through contractors, you can literally hire anyone anywhere. Doing everything long-distance, though, has its own set of challenges.

First, have some sort of contract in place regarding employment. Even if everyone is working speculatively—meaning that they will all get paid when the game is either sold or distributed and has made money—there needs to be something in writing that says that the intellectual property you are creating belongs to the game company. The contract should also lay out the details regarding payment and any provisions regarding termination. The second challenge of working with contractors is related to workflow.

Again, as all the development team members are working in different locales, they will not have the benefit of actually being able to communicate with ease or have meetings to discuss the project. It is important early in the project to establish a means for conferencing, set up collaboration tools, and create a concise pipeline for all of the assets being created. Even though the team is scattered, you should still designate a lead for each department and set up established meeting times for you to conference with them and for them to conference with individual team members.

The easiest method for conducting meetings is to use online video conferencing. There are several companies out there that offer reasonable pricing for this—you may already be using Skype for PC phone calls—and getting the video conference calls up and running is as easy as making sure all concerned have a webcam and headset.

Don't forget to take into consideration any differences in time zones when scheduling meetings. Also, prepare the topics to

Developer Tip

 Most instant messaging programs offer conference call functionality for free! Check out Yahoo! Messenger or Microsoft's Windows Live Messenger for available features and downloads.

discuss in advance so that the call times can be kept low—and stay on that agenda! Keeping the project on track is dependent upon these meetings and the ability for the development team to access collaboration tools. As discussed earlier in the book, the setup and maintenance of a wiki page is the best way for assets to be tracked and for individual team members to be aware of where the project stands. This portal will be the glue that keeps your team together and the shared workspace (not to mention shared drive) for everyone. It's hard to make contractors feel like they are part of a team, so keeping them on point with the overall schedule, concept, and progress helps immensely in that regard.

Of course, the biggest challenge may be just finding people to work within your budget. Where do you find unemployed game developers? There are several places you can begin your search: schools, conferences, and Web sites. Schools are pretty obvious search locations; most students want experience, so you can usually get a certain level of work and commitment out of them with relative ease. This is especially true if they are out of school and unemployed. Most schools have career counselors who can provide you with candidates for employment and even assist you with placement. Just realize that most everyone you acquire from a school is going to be inexperienced (a "noob" or "newbie", if you will). Finding skilled talent will probably require hitting conferences and networking or exploring Web sites that are dedicated to a specific discipline.

Artists, for instance, can be found on Web sites like GFXArtist.com or DigitalArt.org. There are also forums and career sites for programmers, digital producers, and writers that are all a Google search away. Many of them even offer threads that allow you to post jobs and search for available talent. Just be honest when dealing with postings; don't earn a reputation for "bait and switch" tactics regarding employment. Let folks know up front what the situation is and you will be surprised how many people will still want to be involved with your project—especially if you have a strong concept. Just make sure you use nondisclosure agreements (NDAs) when discussing possible employment (more on that in Chapter 14). Don't forget that you can also use recruiters to help with hiring if you are paying your employees.

If you have chosen to scale your first game much smaller or you are located in an area that can support an actual game studio, you may have decided to host a physical location for your company. Once you have found a place within your budget (this includes rent, bills, and the like) and have populated it with the workstations and software tools, it will be up to you to keep enough money flowing into the project to keep the studio functioning. You will also want to take a few additional steps to insure your studio's success.

12.2 Maintaining Your Studio

Getting a development team on board to work with you is only half the challenge. You must also *keep* the development team working for you. Discuss the woes of development with any established studio and the discussion inevitably comes around to turnover and the constant need to hire. So, besides the obvious necessities of maintaining basic operations of the workplace, you must also focus on the things that would be handled by a human resources department at a large studio. Specifically, this means creating a great quality of life.

With game studios all over the world, Ubisoft has made a science out of creating and maintaining a successful studio. Reproduced by permission of UbiSoft. All rights reserved.

Maintaining a quality workplace is not as simple as keeping the hours down—especially when deadlines and milestones become an issue and crunch hours begin creeping up. It also means providing perks and programs that keep the employees happy. As you will probably be working on a limited budget, this requires a lot of planning and ingenuity. Keeping hours down during sprints to a milestone can be as simple as planning and allowing for enough time to get the work done. Meet with the leads (or the most experienced and knowledgeable members of the team) and get as accurate a time estimate as is possible and allow for that amount of time. There's a very small threshold of frustration that employees allow when they are already working for little or no pay.

One of the best ways by which you can keep your development team out of the realm of the frustrated and exasperated is to create and maintain good project management systems. Take a tutorial on Microsoft Project and make sure to use good daily delta reports to keep communication high—especially if you are working only with contractors. The more organized a project is, and the smoother it operates, the better the attitudes will be within the team.

Providing incentives at the workplace can also go a long way towards improving morale at work. Perks can include end-of-week parties at the studio (try and get sponsorship from a local culinary school or brewpub to provide inexpensive treats), a gaming area for breaks (also important for play testing other games on the market), and leniency regarding time off and work schedules. The happier you keep your employees, the longer you will keep your employees—but don't let them run over you! I once worked at very large game developer and publisher that would buy lunch/dinner every day for their employees during crunch time; soon the employees figured out they could ask for more expensive food from better restaurants and the budget for these meals spiraled out of control.

Finally, at the end of the production cycle, when the game is making money, make sure to pay your team what they were promised and offer them the opportunity to work on the next (hopefully funded) project. Don't be another industry horror story; the tales of programmers and artists done wrong by developers are rampant. When you show loyalty to your employees, they show loyalty to you and your company's products.

Once your studio is up and running, it is important to take steps towards creating a grass-roots type of public relations campaign. Because you will not be spending money on a big PR firm to represent your company, you will have to become a little creative in getting your studio's name out there and known.

Development Tip

The International Game Developers Association (IGDA) has a lot of info regarding the quality of life in game studios. Hit their site (http://www.igda.org) for papers on creating a great quality of life at your studio, as well as helpful suggestions for improving working conditions.

12.3 Getting Noticed

The first step in creating a successful public relations campaign is to get your Web site up and running. This can usually be done for little or no money at first: purchase your domain name (easily done through hundreds of hosts like Yahoo!), then create a blog for your company (via Blogger, for example) and have the domain forwarded to it. Wham—you have a site up and running for as little as ten bucks a year! If you feel like spending a little money on the site, you can hire a Web designer (or spend the time designing a site yourself with a program such as Adobe GoLive or Dreamweaver) and purchase an online hosting plan. A bigger, structured site allows for a lot more functionality and information on your Web page—including job postings, press releases, and the ability to download a demo for your game once it becomes available.

The second step in your plan for world domination should involve getting a playable demo available as quickly as

possible—then taking this demo to every gaming conference you can afford and showing it off. Make copies of it and put it in the hands of publishers, gamers, and online distributors. Pay for a stand at trade shows and have the game demo playing behind you (or better yet, available for people to try). Free swag can also go a long way towards driving traffic to you.

Trade advertisement placement in your game (or on your site) to T-shirt companies and printers in exchange for free shirts, stickers, or whatever. This activity puts your company name in the hands of attendees. Every T-shirt, bumper sticker, or hat is a moving billboard for you. Actually attending the conferences also presents a multitude of opportunities to network and spread word of your game and company at parties and mixers (especially the Independent Games Festival and Summit). Another avenue to consider is the use of ads in the trades. Design a nice advertisement and place it in the most popular magazines.

You can purchase advertisements in magazines that focus on video games, Web sites that do the same, and even newspaper ads in cities that feature prominent video game communities. There are lots of different strategies for creating a successful guerilla marketing campaign (check out some of them on GMarketing.com), just be sure you're not crossing the line. Past attempts at guerilla marketing on the streets have created bad situations like bomb scares, hefty fines for pollution (flyers gone awry), and a bad presence in the community due to tasteless ads and billboards. You can see some examples of successful independent games on the Web site IndieGames.com.

While you are making your ad, you should also write a press release that can be sent out to local press. Getting on local television or being featured in a write-up in a local paper is still press. Save all of your press clippings and use them in your media kit when you are pitching perspective publishers.

My final suggestions for getting noticed in the game industry centers around creating mods for existing games. Lots of game designers have gotten their start by taking this avenue of approach and it can work for your company as well. By creating new levels, characters, and so on. for a popular game, you can quickly get noticed by a lot of gamers as well as the game industry.

12.4   Protecting Your Idea

Though this can be a legal issue and we will discuss these in Chapter 3, it's important to touch on this for just a moment. As I mentioned earlier, one of the keys for a successful independent game is to have a great game concept. Once this game concept is honed to fit your budget and schedule, it is important that you protect it. This means only discussing it with your development team (at least initially—later on, you will of course want to discuss it as much as possible for press purposes), using non-disclosure agreements, and licensing your idea as much as is possible. Did you write a script for the game? Register it with the Writer's Guild of America. Are there trademark characters, logos, and so on? Register them.

You may have also made a deal or partnered up with someone to make a game from an existing book, movie, or television program. If you have decided to go this route, you must license (or option) the work for use in your game. This is usually expensive and is not for everyone, but using an already successful piece of intellectual property is a great way to take advantage of existing buzz. As I mentioned before, the final chapter of this book discusses the legal aspects of game creation more, but just know from the onset that you should (at the minimum) protect your idea legally and fundamentally from being copied or stolen. Now let's talk about the game you will be protecting.

12.5   Your Concept

The ideal independent game would (of course) be innovative, fun, illustrate a fair amount of potential for future development—and most of all, cinematic! Putting together a great concept is the first task you have in front of you—and the most important—but nobody can really help you with that if you want to be the game's designer. Here are some suggestions you can follow, though, that will keep you on a trim budget and schedule, as well as keep your chances for completion/success high:

Design for PC. Don't worry about consoles at this stage. Getting dev kits for some consoles is an extremely difficult task (developer kits/consoles are very expensive). If you are going to go console, aim small. This means going the XNA route and designing an arcade-style game for Xbox Live Arcade or designing a Wii game (check out WiiWare).

Come up with a unique feature. Have a game character with never-before-seen skills or abilities and integrate that into the games controls—or offer some level of usability that is unique. Doing all the things we have discussed in this book to make a game cinematic will go a long way towards the immersion and appeal of the game, but coming up with a great feature gamers have never seen will go a long way towards making the game unique and fun.

Maximize the cultural impact of the game. This doesn't mean you should make the game political or anything. It just means that the more people in the world that enjoy the game, the more places you can sell it. Design around themes and styles that are universally accepted and enjoyed.

Minimize the interface. If you need an instruction book for the game, it's probably too complicated. Design so that a gamer can jump right in and start playing.

Design the game to be expanded. Leaving the possibility open for expansion—even if it is just for customization, additional maps, or new characters—means the chance to add on more sales down the line. Great characters, story, and game play also opens the doors for sequels down the line. Also, if the game is successful when released, showing a publisher that the game can get and be much bigger will be a great selling point.

These are just a few basic guidelines to keep in mind when coming up with your concept. Again, if you are using the cinematic techniques discussed in this book, you will also be creating a much richer game experience, even if the game's theme is not massive in scope.

Development Tip

 Noah Falstein, one of the people interviewed in this book, has a Web site called *The Inspiracy* where he discusses rules/ guidelines for a successful game. His aim is to get 400 tips for the game designer (called the 400 Project)! Check out his useful advice at www. theinspiracy.com.

Games like those in the *Splinter Cell* series always start with a strong game concept. Reproduced by permission of UbiSoft. All rights reserved.

Once you know what your game will be and what the major features are, you will want to parcel out a small piece to be developed first into a demo/prototype. If this is done well enough, you can use this demo to pitch the full game to publishers; worse case scenario, you will have a great demo to use for marketing purposes through your site. Make sure you include information regarding your company if you are using the prototype to pitch potential distributors.

In addition to the game design document and the demo, you will want a company mission statement, risk analysis (including an analysis of competition), and estimates regarding scheduling and budget. These are the things you will need when approaching major publishing companies to secure a distribution deal. Once you have put your concept together, gotten your demo finished, and your Web site/studio is up and running, you will want to start attracting the publishers.

12.6   Attracting the Game Industry

We have already discussed a few of the major ways to attract publishers to you: Your Web site, your demo, and creating a high profile at gaming conventions to name a few. Joining the IGDA will help you as well, as they sponsor events during the year, but in the end, you will have to get your company/game name out there. It is rare for a publisher to actively approach and seek out independent game companies and find them. You will have to find them.

Finding the publishers can be accomplished by finding and talking to them at conventions, contacting them through their Web site (sometimes they even have their office numbers on the site), and visiting their actual company locations. Whichever way you get to them, set up a pitch meeting with the studio heads (sometimes a publisher has a head of acquisitions). If they choose to grant you a meeting, you will be given the opportunity to "pitch" to them—or sell them—on the idea of distributing your game. This literally means you stand in front of them and tell them about your game and why they should publish it.

12.7   Using Your Soft Skills

Getting to the pitch meeting though means becoming a pro at the "soft" skills that make a great game producer. In a nutshell, this is the fine art of schmoozing. Networking. Talking people up. Knowing how to communicate with people without being overly pushy is as important as knowing who you should be schmoozing with. I've been to parties at SXSW Interactive conferences and watched young designers talking for hours about their project to a programmer who can basically do nothing for them and their career. I've also seen creative directors (who have had a couple drinks) blathering on about details of their new project that I'm quite sure shouldn't be discussed. This is not a good strategy.

Successful schmoozing means knowing your goals, who can get you to them, and how to speak to them. Your agenda should be obvious. Need name talent on your team? Online distribution? Or just career advice? Okay, good. Now, who can give you what you need? If you're at a conference, there may be a registration book or online resource that tells you who is attending the conference or who they represent. Narrow down the field, get online, see what they look like and what they are currently working on, and find them! If you go to every party at a conference, chances are they will be at one of these. If not, they are probably speaking at the conference; go to their panel and then approach them afterwards.

When you approach someone who can help you, it's always best to talk about them first. Much like the film industry, creative types in the game industry always like talking about their own projects. A quick compliment and innocent query usually gets them talking in no time. Once you have rapport, broach the idea of maybe talking to them after the conference for career advice. This suggestion usually spawns a moment where everyone in the vicinity exchanges business cards. Now you have a quality contact. Thank them for their time and *leave them alone*. Nobody likes being stalked at conferences and harassed. Once the conference has been over a reasonable amount of time (four or five days), send a quick email to remind your contacts who you are and thank them again for helping you (even though they have not done anything yet).

Getting from "hello" to getting your foot in their door is the soft skill that marks most successful producers in the game industry. Once you are comfortable at mixers and talking to complete strangers, consider doing some speaking engagements yourself (if you have something to speak about and your listeners have a reason to listen). The more you are exposed to the general game population, the easier it will be to open doors. Just remember that the golden rule is to always talk to them about *them* and not yourself…at least, not until you are asked. And then, when you are asked about what you are working on, be enthusiastic and brief. Practice coming up with a little two- to three-line teaser about your game (sometimes called an "elevator pitch" in the movie business). Sometimes, this quick spiel alone will get you to the bigger meeting and allow you to do a full pitch to a publisher.

12.8 Learning How to Pitch

There are several different ways to approach a pitch. Some people will tell you to just approach the entire meeting as a casual conversation and simply tell your audience what your game is about, then answer questions about it. Others say that putting on a full-blown show with slides, a poster, demo, and so on is the way to go. Either way, there will be some definite things that a publisher will want to talk about with you—and whether you are telling them or showing them the answers—these have to be discussed.

The highest priority of the conversation will center around the subjects of target audience and marketing. Be prepared to go into great detail about exactly what kind of gamer is going to want to buy your game and how your game differs from the other titles competing for the same dollars. This isn't about explaining the game's story or cool characters; at a pitch meeting, you are quizzed about demographics, numbers, and territories that will sell a lot of units. Be prepared for this! Does this mean you should forego the creative aspects of the game? Absolutely not. Just keep it short, succinct, and direct. Bring the demo if you have it and make a poster if you want to, but definitely prepare and practice your presentation.

The better the game, like *Tom Clancy's Ghost Recon Advanced Warfighter 2*, the easier the game to pitch. Reproduced by permission of UbiSoft. All rights reserved.

Stand in front of your friends (and strangers, if you're able) and give them the pitch. Let them ask questions and practice answering them. Pitching is a stressful situation and the more comfortable you are with speaking in front of people and answering unusual questions about your project, the better you will be. You should also practice several different types of pitches; though having a longer presentation for formal meetings is a must, you should also get down a one-line "high-concept" pitch—the old Hollywood-style pitch where you say something like, "It's

Terminator, but with chipmunks instead of robots." The opportunities to give this type of pitch far outweigh the amount of meetings you'll be able to set up.

When you are crafting your various pitches and putting your ducks in a row, keep these tips in mind:

1. *Be on time.* You may not have the busy schedule that you envision for a big game producer yet, but the people you are pitching to are quite busy, so don't waste their time!

2. *Be professional.* Dress appropriately and have plenty of materials. When you are given the "thumbs-up" for the meeting, ask how many people will be there and what the culture of the company is regarding attire.

3. *Know the pitch's audience.* Do they publish casual games or arcade games? How many games do they handle in a year? Are they the appropriate distribution channel for your game? Again, don't waste their time.

4. *Think visually.* Video games, much like movies, are a visual medium. If you go in with only words, you will bore them. Whether it's a slide show, posters and pictures, or a demo playing, you need something to excite your audience visually.

5. *Be your own cheerleader.* If you're not excited about the project, who will be? Be enthusiastic and positive about your project and you will spread that excitement.

6. *Know the logistics.* As I said previously, know how much your budget is, how long it will take to develop, and what anticipated sales are—and be prepared to back those up with details.

7. *Make sure you fit in.* This is similar to tip #3, but is more about making sure that you are doing something that is familiar to the publisher you're pitching to. If they have done very well at marketing FPS games, then explaining how your shooter fits into their catalog will work heavily in your favor.

8. *Show flexibility.* When the publishers offer criticism or suggestions, be enthusiastic about them. Being able to work with them and building your game around set parameters is something all developers have to learn to do.

9. *Be original.* This doesn't mean going to a pitch meeting with a barbershop quartet and singing the pitch. It means bringing in a poster or demo unlike any they've seen before. It can also mean talking about the features of your game that have not been done elsewhere. Stand out and be different.

10. *Show value.* This is less about the product and more about you. Inevitably, if all is going well, the pitch will shift from being about the game to what you have done

in the past and what kind of work ethic you possess. It's one thing for a publisher to distribute your game, but it's quite another to build a relationship with a developer and create a partnership for future projects.

Follow these suggestions and you will do well at any pitch meeting.

Interview: Richard Rouse III, Game Designer

Richard Rouse III is a game designer and writer who has worked in computer and video game development for more than a decade. Most recently, he has served as Director of Game Design at Midway Games, consulting on a wide range of next-generation titles. Prior to that he was Creative Director and Writer on the hit action/horror title *The Suffering* and its sequel, *The Suffering: Ties That Bind*. Rouse has led the design on a number of other games, including *Centipede 3D, Damage Incorporated,* and *Odyssey: The Legend of Nemesis,* as well as contributing to the design on *Drakan: The Ancients' Gates*. He has written about game design for publications including *Game Developer, SIGGRAPH Computer Graphics, Develop, Gamasutra,* and *Inside Mac Games,* and has lectured on game design at the Game Developer's Conference and the Electronic Entertainment Expo. Rouse's popular and sizable book about game design and development titled *Game Design: Theory & Practice* was released in an expanded second edition in 2004 (Wordware Publishing). More information can be found at his Web site, http://www.paranoidproductions.com.

Richard Rouse

Newman: Using the term "cinematic" when designing a game is not always greeted with enthusiasm. For some, it means more cut-scenes and long-winded speeches from the game characters. What does "cinematic" mean to you?

Rouse: I certainly like to differentiate between adding more cut-scenes and making a game more cinematic. If you look at a well-made film, one of its main qualities is that it feels cohesive. All of its parts fit together. They're of the same tone and basic storytelling style. As a result the viewing experience flows well.

Cinematics can be a useful tool in games, but the reality is that when a cinematic is playing there is no meaningful interaction and the real gameplay has stopped. To me, they make the whole experience of playing the game feel disjointed, with snippets of un-interactivity jammed between the game itself in order to tell a story the player typically has no control over whatsoever. This is why players tend to not like cinematics and complain about the long ones: watching videos is not why they decided to buy a particular game, regardless of how good they may be.

I tend to try to avoid using phrases like "let's make this part of the game more cinematic" because if one is to take that term literally, it would mean to make the game more like a movie and thus less interactive. And surely no one wants that. I've also found that different people use the term to mean wildly different things. Sometimes it does mean more cut-scenes, sometimes it means more immersion, sometimes it means more action set pieces.

But if we must use the term, I prefer to think of ways games can steal specific filmic techniques and make them part of gameplay. The slow-motion effect in *Max Payne* (and recently in *Stranglehold*) is a great example of this: it was based on a technique that players were used to seeing in films and made it interactive. The developers didn't just put slow-motion sections in the cut-scenes, they actually added it to the game itself and made it meaningful and a lot of fun. Simple things like tilting the camera or adding depth of field or using a split screen are all examples that can be applied to gameplay and open up cool new gameplay dynamics. This makes a game more "cinematic" while still definitely a game.

Newman: How can a designer avoid falling into the trap of what you call "Hollywood Envy"?

Rouse: I think I first heard Chris Crawford use this expression, and I've happily appropriated it for my own purposes. Hollywood Envy refers to the sad fact that a lot of people working in games don't see them as "cool" enough and secretly wish they working on films in far sexier and glitzier Hollywood. To make themselves feel closer to the "magic" of Hollywood (or perhaps to act as a portfolio for when they try to switch careers) they tend to copy blindly from films. The most egregious example of this I can think of is scrolling credits at the end of video games, which lack even the interactivity of DVD playback. Can I rewind them? Almost never. Can I even pause them? Hardly ever. Computers are made for presenting data like credits in ways that players could flip through at whatever speed they wanted, if they wanted. Computers are practically made for interactive display of text. But when Hollywood Envy takes hold of someone, you end up with scrolling credits because it's "more like the movies". Now, do credits display systems actually matter that much to games? Of course not. But whenever I see super-long cut-scenes that have my main character doing all manner of cool action moves that would have been better in gameplay (inherently better, as the player would have been in control of them) I fear the team has fallen into the thrall of Hollywood Envy. Designers should always ask themselves, "Am I making this decision because it makes my title a better game? Or just because I secretly wish I were making a movie?"

Newman: It seems that the areas that have benefited the most from cinematic game design have been in the realm of game cinematography and game writing. What are some less-obvious benefits of drawing experience from the film industry?

Rouse: I agree with you about cinematography: there's a lot we can learn about camera techniques from films, from shot framing to how a real camera moves through the world. Borrowing from films seems perfect, as long as people are smart about how to take a specific camera style from a film and make it dynamic and procedural so players are still in control of the experience.

Film writing I actually find to be less directly applicable to game writing. Other than the cut-scenes, game writing is often finding clever ways to convey gameplay-useful and also character/back-story-interesting information during gameplay without breaking the flow. It often means writing as succinctly as possible, even beyond the succinctness you find in films. Games also affect the type of stories one can write: in game development, one typically starts with a set of gameplay constraints and figures out the best way to tell a story in a very limited space. The best game writers can embrace those constraints and write very compelling stories around them, but it's a wholly different way than how movie scripts are created.

I do think there are lot of other areas in which film techniques can be studied and used to enrich games. For instance, in terms of audio mixing, there's a lot of layering going on in films soundtracks that games can continue to learn from. If you look at a Robert Altman film like *M*A*S*H* or *McCabe and Mrs. Miller*, he layers so much information into the soundtrack via characters talking on top of each other that you almost can't get it all in one viewing, which is perfect for games where we want players to be able to explore the story space. Some of the best games have done this successfully, and *BioShock* is a recent example. *BioShock* was also a great example of musical underscoring mixed with in-world licensed audio. The score for that game is quite understated most of the time, to the point where people don't notice it, but it provides exactly the right amount of emotional nuancing to make the player feel specific emotions at different key points of the game progression. The licensed tracks from the 1950s, instead of playing "on the camera" as part of the soundtrack are instead inserted into the environment, helping to set the tone while emerging organically from the world.

I also think there's a lot that games can learn from movies in terms of pacing; manipulating players to anticipate one thing happening, but then springing something entirely different on them. Also, I think films can help make game developers into better editors of content and experience—selecting only the parts that audiences are going to react to the strongest. Hitchcock said films were life with all the dull bits cut out. Some games, like MMOs, tend to be 98 percent dull bits (endless grinding, traveling across great distances, trying to organize a raid). But even single-player action/adventure titles often have dull bits that could be cut out.

Newman: One of the great axioms of screenwriting has always been "Show, don't tell". This seems to be a particularly good rule to use within the game industry. What are some of the ways that a designer can still get the story across to the gamer without the use of heavy dialogue?

Rouse: I don't think I'm the first person to say this, but I subscribe to the principle that you should "Do, don't show". Whenever possible, let the player do things instead of watching them be played out in a cut-scene or in events he can't interact with. Games need to focus on what they do best (letting players interact) and not what they do badly (long complex plots that full apart when you change any part of them). That said, I'm a big fan of using dialog in games, but figuring out ways to integrating it into the play experience. This is something the *System Shock* games did really well; through the audio logs, you could play back at any time while you explored, solved puzzles, had some combat, and so on. The talk radio dialog in the *GTA* games are another great example of this. It helps set the scene, establish the world, let the player know what kind of world he's in, all without taking him out of the play experience. Of course, super-critical dialog may need to be reinforced via mission objectives or forcing players to pay more attention to certain pieces of dialog that are intended to give them direction. But if you're just telling some back story, it's probably okay if players don't hear 100 percent of it. Designers should figure out a way to layer it in the background instead of forcing characters to listen to someone drone on endlessly.

Newman: It seems that great writing is starting to matter more in the game industry. How does a writer balance the need for great plot and conflict without making what you call "an interactive movie"? And does a game need an actual "writer"?

Rouse: Games absolutely do need writers, but writers that understand games and writers that realize they're making a game first and a story second. A game that has great story but lacks compelling gameplay is a failure, while a game with good gameplay and a weak story can still succeed. Games can also limit a lot of what you can do as a writer and what plots will come across well, but limitations can be creatively stimulating instead of stifling, if writers approach them with the right mindset.

Assuming that a project has the right writer, I think they need to be on the project full-time, not just around for a short chunk at the beginning or middle or end. Someone on the team needs to be the eternal champion of the story, even if they don't necessarily write the dialog or even come up with the plot. But this story champion needs to be present at all stages (just like a lead designer or a lead artist are on the project the whole time) to make sure that the game's story is at least considered in all decisions. This person may also be the lead designer or the lead level designer or have other responsibilities on the project, but they're the guy everyone turns to with story questions.

Decisions about the story and requests for revisions happen throughout the project, and someone with a good story sense needs to be present to make sure those are done correctly. Sure, a given game-play encounter might be more fun if it were flooded with lava, but does that make any sense with the plot? Is the damage to the story less than the increase in the fun gained by adding the lava? And if the lava really is a lot of fun, how can the story be altered to support that? This is a ridiculous example of course, but there are a million smaller decisions that are made over the lifetime of a project. Having a story champion present is absolutely essential to make sure that a sensible, well-written story survives amidst all the changes.

Newman: In your opinion, does the game industry spend enough time working in preproduction? It seems there are a number of current games hitting the shelves that would have benefited from spending more time dealing with choices such as locations, lighting, plot, and so on during the concept phase.

Rouse: Not spending enough time in preproduction is a huge problem. As soon as there's the smallest hint of a cool game, publishers often want it out as soon as possible, creating an unproductive race for the finish line that typically involves throwing too many people on a project way too soon. Perhaps because they've been working at it so much longer, Hollywood is much smarter about this. Once a movie starts shooting, delays and over-runs are a much rarer thing than they are in the game industry. But at the same time I wouldn't say that the average movie is better than the average game because of that.

But yes, definitely, most games could benefit in more time in preproduction. That's the time when you should prove out all the major gameplay risks, implementing anything that's remotely unknown on the project, getting your pipeline working, and, yes, getting a plot and parts of a script in place that everyone's happy with. Of course, it will continue to change over the course of development, but you need to have your best attempt at the story pretty early on.

Newman: Midway Games brought in director John Woo for the game *Stranglehold* last year. In your experience, do film directors grasp the concepts of interactivity immediately? Describe the process of working with a film director on a game.

Rouse: I'm not going to reference any one person it particular, but in my experience people who have worked only in film typically do not immediately grasp how games work. Often they're the first to admit that, and they come to these relationships ready to learn a lot and work collaboratively. What directors are good at is thinking outside the box a bit more: because they don't know much about games, a lot of their ideas are all over the place and hard to use, but some of them are brilliant and fit perfectly with games. The trick is getting a film director to work with a game team that's experienced and can help filter those ideas—cherry-picking the best ones, if you will. There's a lot of back and forth, but in the end it's still the game teams doing the vast majority of the work. But getting in other creative forces can definitely be a very positive thing for the game, as long as you harness that creativity properly.

Newman: More and more, we are seeing a lot of simultaneous game and film releases (especially with animated films like *Ant Bully* and *Bee Movie*). Do you think the possibility of crossover appeal helps or hurts the game industry?

Rouse: In most of the cases where films and games that ship simultaneously, the game is done in a huge hurry under huge constraints. Sometimes this can lead to really cool little games, but more often it leads to something that feels very derivative and rushed. The motivations for doing these games are almost never creative—they're financial. If you're doing one of those games you're riding on the coat-tails of cross-media "event" that surrounds the launch of the film and trying to sell some games starring a CG movie character in the same way McDonald's is trying to sell some extra hamburgers branded with that same CG movie character. As I say, there are lots of people who manage to make nifty games in these situations, and there's nothing wrong with trying But I'm not sure it's something that makes the industry stronger creatively.

That said, there are also some movie games that are done right, where the development teams don't have to stick to the moving target of a film script and where they have enough time to really get the game right. But these are still the exception, not the rule.

Newman: What elements would you look for in a game, if you were going to option one for a movie?

Rouse: There are two types of licenses in Hollywood: ones where the license is already a Big Property and has a built in fan base that will go see the film version (such as *Harry Potter*, *Mortal Kombat*, and *The DaVinci Code*). However, the vast majority of properties Hollywood licenses are not very big before Hollywood gets hold of them. A lot of movies are adaptations from books that have been read by 100,000 people at most. If a Hollywood movie gets only 100,000 people to buy tickets, it's a big flop. So for this second category of licenses, some Hollywood producer really likes the story or characters involved in that property and think they can turn it into a much more financially successful film; in essence, making the IP [intellectual property] much more popular by making it a movie. Games, on the other hand, tend to license properties (like the examples you cited) in the hopes that some subset of the people who went to see the movie will go buy the game. If they get one-tenth of the film goers to buy the game, they're making a tidy profit. It's more rare (though not unheard of) for games to take a small book or an obscure board game and try to make it into a huge game. It's still true that Hollywood is far more the entertainment taste-maker for the country than games are, and the realities of these different licensing efforts show that.

The trick with optioning a game to make into a movie is that the game has to have an identity that is unique to it. A lot of games, despite being fantastic game experiences, once you remove the game play have fairly standard/derivative settings and characters. How many games have "space marines" in them? Hollywood already has a space marines property (the *Alien* movies), and it doesn't need to license something from games to get another one. I think that games could benefit from coming up with more original characters, worlds, and stories. It's great to draw some inspiration from movies or books or whatever, but too many games just copy the setting/theme/tone from a popular work in another medium and call it done. The best films or novels or games are the ones that make a setting that really stands on its own. Beyond just making sure that the game property could work as a two-hour feature, if I were optioning a game for a movie, I'd look for something that had its own distinct identity and that would still stand up once you removed the game play.

13

THE GAME BUSINESS

Like all business, the game industry thrives upon sales and marketing. As a beginning game producer, you may define your personal success as finishing a project or creating a new or innovative feature that has never been explored before, but the majority of game developers and publishers use sales to determine success. Making a marketable game on time and budget will ensure financial and commercial success.

The business plan for your company and your first game should be built around the concept of "sales numbers"—in other words, you must sell a lot of games. This figure is not the same thing as how much money you will make. That number will be calculated after you have paid for the cost of development and marketing. Usually, the demand of the consumer is the factor that determines your place in the market (how much your game sells for). If your game has to be sold for a dollar as a download to get your sales numbers up, then that will be your eventual position. Generating huge numbers (in sales and revenue) will give you the stats and leverage you will need when you pitch your next title to a bigger publisher.

There is an axiom in the movie industry—coined by famous film teacher Dov S-S Simens in his book *Reel to Deal* (Grand Central Publishing, 2003)—that says if you want to make a $20 million movie, first you have to make a $2 million movie. But to make a $2 million movie, you should probably have produced a $200,000 movie. See a pattern here? The same is true for the game industry. Scale low, then slowly work your way up the development food chain to get your game studio on the right track without overtaxing your resources.

Your first step in getting that initial game out the door is to get your business plan, mission statement, and risk analysis in place.

13.1 Business Plan

There are several different types of business plans—most focus on either how your overall company will function or how an individual project will be managed. Because you will have created your concept package that already includes financial information regarding the game (primarily the budget and schedule), you now need a business plan that specifies how you will make your game studio successful. The best way to do this is to define your goals.

New games, like *Call of Duty 4: Modern Warfare*, are very hush-hush during development. Reproduced by permission of Activision. All rights reserved.

Once you have listed the goals of your company—these probably include getting your first game produced, getting an office, and so on—explain how you will get there. Just remember the audience for your business plan! If this is something you are going to take to banks for loan purposes, there are specific things to include in the plan for that—specifically, financial information. Another reason for defining your business plan's audience centers around the idea of secrecy; as you won't be able to get NDAs from casual readers, make sure that your business plan does not have any information in it that needs to remain confidential—especially if you are going to make your business plan public on your Web site.

In a nutshell, a business plan is about defining your goals, how you are going to implement them, and crafting your plan around the intended audience. To this end, you can also create several different versions of your business plan, focusing on what you want the public to know and what you want investors/partners to be aware of. Once you have created your business plan, you can then move on to your company's mission statement and your game's risk analysis.

Production Tip

The Service Corps of Retired Executives offers tons of free advice on their Web site for new startups. They even have local chapters that can help you by answering questions regarding area-specific concerns. Check them out at http://www.score.org.

13.2   Mission Statement and Risk Analysis

When you are putting together the information that you need to get your company up and running—whether it's for incorporating or simply filing a DBA form (Doing Business As—This is the legal document you file that states you are creating a new company, but are not ready to incorporate yet.)—one of the most basic things you need is a "mission statement". This document lays out the basic intentions of your company and your philosophy for business. Most often, there are also clauses within the mission statement that focus on uniting the vision of everyone working with you and address concerns that any business partners may have when doing business with the company.

If you are careful and concise with constructing your mission statement, it will be an important document when soliciting investments, small business loans, and making deals with publishers. It can also serve as a kind of compass within your workplace when resolving differences between employees, hiring new people to join the team, and making decisions regarding the company. The mission statement, along with the risk analysis, will be in the package you take with you when pitching your game to various publishers and distributors.

A "risk analysis" is a report that takes into consideration the various factors involved with creating a game. These factors are broken down into a most likely situation (also called a "proposed scenario"), a worst-case scenario, and a best-case scenario. These three different outlooks illustrate how the title will fare if it sells at expectation, fails to sell enough units to meet that expectation, or sells higher than expected. In addition to these three different outlooks, a risk analysis also includes information regarding the investment: there will be a number that reflects how many copies of the game must be sold to make back the money put into the game, and what price the game will have to sell at as well.

When you are putting together the numbers for the different scenarios, you will want to decide how big a margin of difference to allow for. Game developers can estimate anywhere between 25 to 50 percent differences between the worst- and best-case scenarios. Usually, it's safer to go with the higher percentage—it's better to prepare for the worst than to be sideswiped by it.

Once all of this has been computed and the spreadsheet is formulated, you will have an extremely clear-cut image of what you must do in order for the game to become a successful title. Of course, you must realize that things change during production and your estimates may go up or down. Realizing this early, and modifying your risk analysis at that point, will go a long way to help with getting your final price and units that must be sold computed for the marketing team.

13.3   Crossover Appeal

Perhaps one of the greatest advantages to making a cinematic game is the potential for crossing over into the many other areas of the entertainment industry. Creating a strong story and characters in your game, as well as producing your game using sound cinematography, will make a product that shows potential for films, books, television, and so on. A great example is the whole circus surrounding Bungie Studio's *Halo 3* (well, the whole *Halo* series actually). Characters like the Master Chief are not just "thought up". They are crafted. Carefully. As I am writing this chapter, in addition to the *Halo* games, there are several novels on the shelves, tons of *Halo* toys and merchandise floating around, and a movie in development.

When *Halo 3* hit the shelves, there were also T-shirts, key chains, posters, and tons of other merchandise. Copyright © Bungie LLC and/or its suppliers. All rights reserved.

Getting the appeal of the game to a point where these other projects are possible is as simple (or hard) as creating a strong, cinematic game. When you have the fan base to support branching out into other mediums, you can then decide whether it is financially viable to attempt selling your intellectual property (IP) to those other avenues of sales. Again, make sure to use an attorney when making these deals; as it requires others to license your IP to make toys, books, and other merchandise, you need a lawyer to design and review those contracts.

13.4   Success with Marketing

If you are fortunate enough to make a sale to a publisher, you will get to know their marketing department really well. In many ways, they function as a kind of accountant in the publishing world—they are concerned with getting sales up and maximizing the potential for sales through sound marketing techniques. If you are publishing your own game and using alternative distribution channels, you function (for the most part) as your own marketing department, so it's important that you understand at least basic marketing strategies.

Creating a successful marketing campaign starts as soon as you begin production. If you have created your risk analysis, you should have an idea of the price point you will place on the game. Thus, you can look at other games hitting the market at the same time as yours and determine whether you are creating a competitive title. Coming into the game market at the right time with the right price can make or break your game. If there's a lot of competition scheduled to be released at the same time as your game, it's probably in your best interest to move your date.

The marketing campaigns behind games like *Lord of the Rings Online* from Turbine can be huge and last for years. The artwork appearing to the left is copyright protected and reproduced with permission. © 2008 Turbine, Inc. All rights reserved. This publication is in no way endorsed or sponsored by Turbine, Inc. or its licensors.

The second marketing concern to address is getting word of your product out on the street: generating press. There are several different avenues of approach you can take—and you should take them all—including interviews and articles in trade magazines, reviews, and the use of screenshots. As soon as you are able to do so, you should start getting screenshots of your game together. You can send these out almost immediately to the various online gaming sites like GamingTrend and Gamasutra as previews for your new title and start generating word-of-mouth advertising.

Once you are well into the production cycle, and completion of the game is imminent, you can then try to set up interviews with trade magazines like *Game Developer* and fan-based mags such as *Game Informer*. This process will increase awareness of your game and prime the market for your game's entry. Then, just before the game's release, send out copies of the game to magazines and sites to review. This step provides a last-minute boost (along with any ads you place for your game) to your marketing campaign.

Other major marketing tools at your disposal include the use of your demo, creating a strategy guide (it doesn't have to be a formal, published one—make a nice walkthrough with tips and cheats and put it on your site as a download), and doing presentations. Putting together a program that includes an overview of the game, visuals (concept art, demo, and so on), and other game assets is a great idea for generating foot traffic at conferences and for speaking at conventions.

Once the playable demo is up and running, getting it out there at the conferences (along with you as the spokesman), on your site, and bundled with other games being released is a great way to put your product in the hands of gamers. The higher the visibility your title has in the public's eye, the higher your sales will be—and you will need the revenue to help offset the money you have already spent on development and production. Of course, there are other ways to help lower your bottom line as well, as explained in the following section.

Thousands of gamers picked up the demo/trial version of *The Lord of the Rings Online Shadows of Angmar, Book 12: The Ashen Wastes* when it became available. The artwork appearing to the right is copyright protected and reproduced with permission. © 2008 Turbine, Inc. All rights reserved. This publication is in no way endorsed or sponsored by Turbine, Inc. or its licensors.

13.5   Incentives and Fundraising

In the film industry, states are constantly competing for business dollars—luring film production companies to shoot their movies within their borders. To do this, they usually offer an "incentive package" to film producers. These incentives can include getting a discount on taxes for labor or goods, rebates on total production costs, and discounted or free permits for shooting on location. These incentives can add up to millions of dollars in savings for a film production. Some larger cities even have additional incentives that are offered for setting up shop within their city limits.

Recently, states have taken an interest in providing incentives for game productions as well. The state of Texas has now included incentives for game companies—much like the ones they offer for film productions—to move to Texas to produce their games. Austin is one of the biggest game cities in the country! Other cities and states are have similar programs in progress. If you're in the position to set up shop anywhere in the country—or at least to move to an area offering incentives—this is a great way to lower your overall costs on production. However, if money is a huge issue—or if you are not in the position to move—and you are truly going the guerilla production route, being creative with the use of fundraisers may be the ticket to get your initial revenue.

Fundraisers can be as simple as making T-shirts and selling them or as complicated as setting up a mixer at a popular bar (with donated food and drinks). There are literally hundreds of ways to raise money for a project, and many great books have been written on the subject. Getting a couple of good fundraising projects rolling can get you the startup money you may need to incorporate, buy the software you need, and pay for a good Web site. You probably will not be able to completely fund your project using fundraisers (unless you are on a very low budget), but many people in the film industry have used this tool to get an independent project up and running.

Production Tip

The Texas Film Commission's Web site has a whole section on the game industry and incentives offered in the state. Visit them at http://www.governor.state.tx.us/divisions/film/game/index_html for more information about what you can expect from a production there.

13.6   Publishing 101

Getting a publisher on-board to purchase your game and distribute it is the ultimate goal when producing a game, so this tends to be the number one concern with new, independent game studios. The best way to get a publisher is pretty obvious: create an awesome game. Knowing how to pitch your game and how to set up formal meetings are also important, but in the end, it's all about the game. Creating a cinematic game with awesome game play should be your number one goal from the onset.

Once your awesome game is up and running, the next step is to use those soft skills and go on a mad pitching spree. Hopefully, after you have made the circuit through the major publishers in the game industry, you will have gotten your feet in the doors of a lot of important people and given them your presentation. This process should at least put you in consideration for publishing—or at least given you lots of experience pitching at this point.

If you do get a publisher on board and you sell your game, congratulations! You will be well paid for a job well done. However, if you do not manage to secure a publisher, don't despair! There are several different ways you can self-publish your game without going bankrupt in the process: You can use pure distributors to get your game on shelves or you can go to a digital download or online distributor to sell your game.

Even big titles like Ubisoft's *Tom Clancy's Rainbow Six Vegas 2* uses digital distribution and downloads to get playable maps and add-ons out to gamers. Reproduced by permission of UbiSoft. All rights reserved.

As far as distributors go, there are companies that have made deals with multiple retail chains and have the ability to get your game on the shelves of a lot of stores. Sometimes certain stores have their own submission process to put your product on shelves directly through them as well. Although using a distributor saves you the legwork involved with making deals with all the various stores that will carry your product, a distributor will take a certain percentage of your sales, so consider that before making any final decisions. Also, any distributor or retail chain will want the finished product in hand—this means that you have to find a duplicator to make copies of your game and then print all the materials that go with it (box, instruction manual, cover art, and so on). This can be a pretty big expense—and one you need to allow for from the onset of development if you are going to go this route. Once you have secured deals with retailers and/or distributors (or you have decided to bypass this process), you can then look into the expanding world of digital distribution.

There are many Web sites that specialize in selling game downloads directly to consumers—turn to these places if you don't want to be encumbered with the expense of duplicating your game and printing materials. They usually charge a fee for hosting your game and then (sometimes) get a small percentage of the download price. By going the digital route, you save on your overhead and therefore are able to have a lower price point for your product, which makes your game more competitive in the market. You can also consider selling your game directly from your site; if you've spent the money on a great Web site, you can host the download there and charge folks using a method like PayPal (it's easy and quick to set up an account with them). Going this way means that all the sales go directly into your pocket! The downside, though, is that you are responsible for driving gamers to your site, whereas a bigger site like Steam or Xbox Live Arcade already has a lot of hits and visitors.

Whichever method you take (or if you take both), just remember that there are also foreign markets. With a little research, or the use of a good game attorney, you should be able to identify distributors within other countries that can market and sell your game—if your game is localized enough for sales there. Getting into certain territories may mean going back and opening your closing kit to do a localization. This can be expensive, so make sure that you are going to make money before you do this. There are quite a few places that you can sell an English version of your game without having to go that route.

Another good thing to keep in mind is that most major game developers/publishers consider a game to be successful at around 350,000 copies sold. As you will work at a lower budget than most of them, you will not have to achieve such a sales number to regard your game as a success; but if you do hit this sales number, this is a great selling point to make sure to mention when you are pitching your next game.

Life as an independent developer and publisher is tough, but rewarding. As an independent producer, gamers look to you for new and innovative approaches to gaming, as well as inspiration for their own ideas. Get out there and meet others in your position and learn what they are doing—if the independent community can't help each other, who can?

Production Tip

As you develop your game, there are lots of people doing exactly what you are. As a result, many commercial game studios now offer developer's programs for up-and-coming game producers. Check out GarageGames' Affiliated Developers program (http://www.garagegames.com) as an example of this type of program.

Production Tip

Lots of advice and information for independent developers can be found at Indie Games' Web site (http://www.indiegames.com). Get educated and get a leg up on the competition.

Patrick Hamilton

Interview: Patrick Hamilton, President of Wardog Studios

Patrick Hamilton has been in the computer field for close to fifteen years with emphasis in information technology and security. He has an MS in Network Security and a BS: Information Technology with a minor in Computer Science. He served in the U.S. Navy as an Aegis Fire-Control and was part of the precommissioning crew of the *USS Milius* (DDG-69). He believes that a niche market exists for sophisticated games, which can support additional media and business capabilities, as well as to finally release his long awaited mech system into the gaming community.

Newman: Is it still possible to make an "independent" game?
Hamilton: Yes it is, even for an MMOG. The Internet provides the means for individuals, teams, and companies to have global reach without the worry or hassle of retail distribution. Although digital distribution has not been as accepting as to retail distribution in the past, this is no longer the case. I believe that both forms of distribution are about even and digital will shortly overcome retail.

Producing an MMOG may seem impossible, in that large teams or large budgets are required. The budgeting of new MMOGs seems to keep going up in the millions each year—even as expensive as a full-feature film. I will state this: this is not the case, nor has it ever been. Small teams with small budgets can produce successful MMOGs without the need for going to publishers. Producing online games in the multimillion-dollars range is not the right direction. Looking at the computer and IT fields, technology is supposed to make things be better, go faster, and cost less. In the MMOG sector, this does not seem to be the case, so research is needed to figure out what is going wrong and how to exploit it. This is where smaller teams have an advantage to create new paradigms in how such games are created and released.

The MMOG market is a young sector and has plenty of room of growth. There are three strong advantages of MMOGs and those are as follows. MMOGs are living games, with a much longer shelf life than that of conventional games. Thus it is possible to build the core system first and then expand over time, implementing phases (called a Phased Approach) for the release of the full game. Lower-resolution graphics are needed due to performance issues (though this will change as technology improves), allowing teams to create games without the worry of using the latest and greatest graphics possible. And by having a global reach, there is bound to be a viable market for a particular title.

Newman: Recently, EA acquired BioWare/Pandemic. The more smaller studios that are snatched up by big publishers, the harder it seems for an independent studio to succeed. What's the key to getting an indie studio up and rolling?

Hamilton: I would say that the key to getting a studio up and rolling is to first and foremost draft and complete the business plan, not the game design document. Games require money to create to generate revenue. A game must be sellable and the definition of "success" to a developer, team, or studio is needed. Success can be selling just a total of 50,000 copies over a period of one year, or maybe 500,000 units. The business plan will determine that. Additionally, the business plan will help in figuring out the right market and audience to target and identify competitors, and will help secure funding from potential investors. Even if a team is to develop a game for nonprofit use, a business plan is still needed to help show the expenses and how they would be covered.

The second key is what is going to be the innovation, that uniqueness that the game will have compared to others? This innovation or hook does not need to be in the technical programming side of things: it can be of game mechanics, level of sophistication, cinematic, or blending in other forms of media or technology. Small studios tend to have the freedom to be creative and innovative, while large studios and big publishers become more conservative. The big companies rarely want to take on more risk than is needed when millions of dollars are at stake.

When pitching to investors, again, the game needs to be sellable. What features or concepts does it have that will make an investor want to sign a check right away? The best angle that I have observed has been to add in business capabilities and refer to our project as a form of business entertainment system, rather than a game. Trying to get investors for a game is hard, because the word "game" implies a high-risk venture with which many other game projects are competing. When talking with potential investors, I did not receive much of a good reaction when talking about a new game; however, when talking about a massive virtual interactive service that blends in other forms of media and business capabilities, such as in-world Web browsing and product placement, the interest has been much favorable.

Newman: With game development teams getting larger and more expensive to maintain, it seems that a new development model is needed. Is it more cost-effective to maintain a "permanent" team at the studio, or to turn to contractors for the bulk of the work?

Hamilton: I would say that using both is the way to go. Have a core team to work on the critical systems and the creativity of the game, while contractors perform the bulk or take care of the mundane side of things. Typically, outsourcing to other specialized companies is a cost savings. However, take the time to conduct due diligence when dealing with other companies. See what they can do: provide some sample work for them to do and see what the results are.

Newman: There's been a lot of talk about game projects essentially being treated and managed like a film project—meaning that a team is assembled for a specific game, the game is created, then the team is disbanded. Is this a good development model?

Hamilton: The ideal method is to start with a small team—if possible, with third-party companies or contractors to help keep the cost down. As more funding is secured with later rounds or approaching launch, slowly grow the team, but not much—only what is needed. When the game has been launched, then grow the team to match the revenue earned. This is to help provide additional content to grow the game, as well as to begin work on another project if so desired. Avoid developing a game with a large team, launching the game, and then laying off employees. That may be typical in the game industry, but not with MMOGs; that is a sign of mismanagement and of conventional thinking. MMOGs are not the same as conventional computer games and require their own form of development model. Unlike conventional computer games, MMOGs are living games, able to be added onto, changed, and upgraded.

Newman: What impact does the choice of game engine have on a game budget?

Hamilton: The game engine has one of the most significant impacts for the budget and generally requires an upfront cost. Also, the game engine will provide additional capabilities and limitations that may have not been considered for designing a game. For example, Game Engine X cannot support aircraft speeds past 250 mph when using 1:1 scale. So either some creativity will be needed, such as changing the scale, writing up some fictional reasons as to why, or using descriptive words instead of numbers.

I believe that there are three choices:

1. Build the engine.
2. Take an open source engine or platform and build upon it.
3. License one.

Each choice has its pros and cons. Of the three, I recommend licensing one, even if on a budget that requires creativity. The reason for this is that building an engine or platform from scratch or from an existing one is a challenging endeavor that will take one to three (or more) years to complete. During that time, the engine may become severely out-of-date before it is completed. I recommend taking this approach only if the team has the expertise to design, document, and develop a complex system. Licensing an engine or platform is the better choice, in my opinion, as another company is dedicated to only building that engine or platform.

If I may add to this, something that I have noticed with teams and companies is going for the best and most expensive engine or platform to use, which will then solve the majority of problems and the game will sell big. This is also assuming that multimillion-dollar funding (even at $2 million) is going to be easy to obtain. I consider this a mind trap, as every engine has its problems and quirks. Additionally, securing the funding to purchase such engines is rare, and best to start with an affordable one and get the project rolling.

Newman: Today, most games are financed by a publisher, which means that most independent studios work with an extremely constricted budget. How difficult is it for a studio to finance a game, much like a film, by going through a bank?

Hamilton: It is difficult, no doubt about it, but securing funding is should be thought of in terms of, "Not if, but when." Stay positive and keep going. If funding has not been secured by a certain period, then reassess why this has happened, make the needed changes, and keep going. Also, acquiring funding takes time and action; it will not happen without effort being made. From what I have experienced, it is best to find a private investor (angel investor) to gain the seed money to grow the game from a "tech demo" into a workable game, though not a full-blown environment. Funding by banks is unlikely to happen, in that banks generally only put in money at a dollar per dollar match. Thus if a studio needs $500,000, the bank will provide $250,000 only if the studio can supply the other $250,000. Venture capitalists generally are interested in projects above $5 million and want to see mainly two items: the experience of the management and the potential of the revenue generated from the idea.

Newman: Is the use of completion bonds getting widespread attention at this point in the game industry? What about the use of "gap financiers"?

Hamilton: I can't really say for the computer game industry, with the use of bonds and gap financiers as whole, but in terms of indie studios, there is not much widespread use. The difficulties with a small game studio are about the same for a small film studio— either a lack of cash available (or funding acquired) and the amount of experience. I believe that over time, the ability to obtain the financing or bonds to ensure the completion of a game project by a small studio will become easier, as the gaming industry is a growing entertainment market. We're still in the early stages of the ability to blend games with films.

Newman: Austin, Texas, has done a great job with implementing local incentives for game productions to get up and running there. Right now, they are offering a grant equal to 5 percent of in-state spending, including wages paid to Texas residents and certain sales tax exemptions for game productions. Will we see more "film incentive"–type programs in the future? Is this enough of an impact upon a game's budget to warrant relocating a studio?
Hamilton: I think it is a given that films and games will become more integrated with each other, even to the point that the interactive system (the game) affects how the film turns out. The computer gaming industry is growing and has exceeded the filming industry (box office, excluding DVD sales) and so it seems to make sense. Also, Web distribution allows for films to be provided to the public; the difficulty for such films is to market to an audience. A gaming community will help provide this targeted audience for Web-distributed films—especially if the film is short and related to the game.

For the incentive for relocating to Austin…I think that does have a strong consideration. It is strong enough for me to reconsider and investigate that possibility.

Newman: In your experience, what have been some of the best marketing strategies involved with selling a game? How about the worst?
Hamilton: The best for us would be partnering up with The Multiverse Network's (http://www.multiverse.net) game portal system. We have been able to be part of the press releases of Multiverse, as well as attending game developer conventions. Multiverse provides a MMOG platform and also a portal. Although a portal with a listing of additional games might seem bring on more competition and detract potential users, I believe this to not be the case. Providing multiple games draws in more users, and those with great success will of course draw in more. Even though users may be playing another studio's game, they may look over the list to find one that is more of what they want, or when they do get bored with a particular game, they may move on over to another one. By being a developer with Multiverse, we have gained some recognition and a following.

For the worst strategy, we haven't made a bad move yet in my opinion. Although being listed on a public gaming Web site, MMORPG.com (http://www.mmorpg.com) was risky, given that our level of graphics in the presenting screenshots looked dated, the results turned out decent. Sure, there was some criticism given, but there are those gamers out there who are willing to look past the graphics to see how the game will play and its mechanics. I also took this risk to test the waters of the public, to be honest with the community, and to show that improvements are occurring. For example, here is the base-line level of graphics, and then some time later, here is another round of screenshots with graphical improvements.

Newman: Does the concept of "crossing over" into the film, book, and merchandise arenas come up when developing a new game concept? What kind of impact does it have concerning key development decisions?

Hamilton: "Crossing over" does have an influence in our designing, which I would assume would be true for others. For novels and films, there does need to be continuity with what is provided in films, novels, and the game. For example, some game systems have the ability for characters to clone after death, thus avoiding death; but how does such a concept get portrayed in novels or films? Often cloning is ignored, and deaths of characters occur; but yet characters can't die permanently in the game?

The amount of impact in my opinion is strong, but in the game industry in general, it appears to not be a concern that the game system is done differently with films and novels, and by so doing, heated debates occur with the fan base of the IP. What is seen in a film or read in a book should be portrayed as close as possible within a game environment, and vice versa. Also the game environment of a MMO needs to change over time, hopefully in a dynamic way in which the actions of players have an impact. To maintain a static environment is much like having a theme park with rides that never changes. This doesn't breathe in much new life into books or films; this would cause a loss of interest with the fan base. Much interest would be generated if a person knew that what he or she was doing would have an impact with the game world, which in turn could be portrayed in a future book or film ("Hey, that's my character in the movie!") would have a profound impact, I believe.

Merchandising is on the easier side for, say, clothes and figures. As MMOGs use 3D models, those models can be used for plastic models or figures. I would say the difficulty with that is finding a good partner to work with and handle the selling of the merchandise; the rest is easy after that.

Newman: How accessible are publishers? How can a developer maximize a pitch to them?

Hamilton: At first, when starting our project, I thought that the plan would be to create the documents, make a short presentation, and then pitch the concept to publishers. After talking to a few publishers' representatives, I have found out that to win a deal with a publisher is tough for the following reasons: The team or company must have made about five to eight games, therefore providing experience; the game idea must have the potential to sell a million copies; you must be willing to sign away the rights of your team's IP to the publisher (that is, you no longer own the game, the story, and so on)—over 80 percent of the game design will be changed by the publisher; you must be willing to accept a cut of 10 to 20 percent of net sales (minus cost overheads and other things), with the low teens expected for the first timers; and you must be willing to work on other projects by the publisher, as your project will be contracted out to other developer studios.

In all honesty, the best way to release a game is the self-publishing route. This is possible and profitable today, as electronic distribution is gaining wide acceptance. The publishers' only form of control is through retail distribution, and successful titles no longer require retail distribution. Self-publishing is tough, but possible, and viral marketing through the Internet is not as difficult as it would seem. Gamers are Internet-savvy and use the Internet extensively.

Newman: What advice would you give a new studio trying to compete with the "big boys"?

Hamilton: Find a niche market or make the game fit into a niche market. "Niche" is not a bad word; niche marketing is how small companies compete with big companies. Go for a smaller targeted audience, which should prove to be more loyal than the mass-targeted audience.

MMOs are still young and can be made by a few people or a small team with a creative budget. It is possible and has been done. The group I work with is an example of it. Do not let others tell you that only big teams and millions of dollars are needed to make MMOs. "Gone are the days of single programmers or small teams making games." I have heard and read that line of text since I owned a Commodore home computer in the 1980s, and yet games are being made by a single programmer or small teams to this day. A new MMO just needs one person, one idea to get it started. You've got to start somewhere—and never give up!

LEGAL ISSUES

14.1   Intellectual Property

The code, art, and other elements that make up a game are not tangible items like, say, a car. They are known as "intellectual property" (IP). This goes for stories, concepts, and so on. A very specific branch of law deals with intellectual property and lawyers who specialize in it will be the folks to turn to when you discuss publishing or distributing your game. Selling your game to a publisher means that you are also selling the IP involved with the game. All of this must be laid out in the contracts involved with publishing.

Another factor regarding IP in your game involves the individual employees working for you. Make sure that it is written in

An example of character art developed for *Lost Planet: Extreme Condition.* Reproduced by permission of Capcom U.S.A., Inc. All rights reserved.

their employee contracts that all IP made by them (code, art, and so on) belongs to the company. If you have not done this, you probably will not get a deal with a publisher—they will not want to deal with ownership issues down the line.

Contracts are just one way that intellectual property laws affect you. Piracy laws are also in place to make sure that your property is not stolen or improperly licensed. In addition to protecting you, IP law also protects others—you may have to license IP from other people as well. If you use other people's music in your game or if you are basing your game on a book or movie, you will have to license that for your game. An attorney is the best person to make this happen.

Legally, one of the first steps to take to protect your game is to file any copyrights or trademarks.

14.2   Copyrights and Trademarks

Copyrights are used throughout the world to protect an original piece of work from being stolen or illegally used by someone else. They can be obtained for everything from books to music to pieces of art to programs. The main thing to understand about copyrights is that they can protect only tangible items. You cannot copyright an idea. This means that although you still have a great idea, it's probably not a good idea for a lot of people to know about it! Once you have created something from your idea, it is protected—and the good thing is, it's protected right then. Registering your copyright is something that you should definitely do, but the law says that you are protected from the moment you have created your product.

When you are working on your independent game, make sure that everyone involved understands and assigns the copyright for the game to you (or the company). No publisher or distribution channel will take the time to consider your title if you do not possess ownership of the game and all copyrights and trademarks involved.

Trademarks work a little differently than a copyright. Trademarks are usually identifying symbols, logos, or marks that represent your company or game. Once you have set up your company and come up with a suitable logo, you will brand your game with this logo—essentially giving it your stamp of ownership. By registering your trademarks for your company and game, you protect yourself from other people who may try to capitalize upon your name or products. Make your logos distinguishable from similar names and concepts and to try to use uncommon spellings or words. As there are many different types of trademarks, research what category your items fall under before getting them registered.

Assassin's Creed main character Altair is unique enough to require a trademark for merchandising purposes. Reproduced by permission of UbiSoft. All rights reserved.

Using trademarks and copyrights is one of the most basic ways to protect your game from theft. Research use of copy protection in your game so that it is difficult to copy and pirate. Though a school of thought regarding piracy is that it is free advertising (and increases word-of-mouth buzz), just know you can take steps to protect your game (it will just take time and money that could be spent on other areas of the game).

Development Tip

The United States Patent and Trademark Office has an official Web site for registering your trademark. Check them out at http://www.uspto.gov.

14.3   Nondisclosure Agreements and Contracts

As mentioned earlier, keeping a lockdown on your concept is of the utmost importance early on in development. The most basic form, which you will get to know very well in this regard, is the Nondisclosure Agreement (NDA)—the agreement that swears everyone working on your project to secrecy. You will use this when discussing the title with potential employees, external vendors, and everyone at the company. The only hitch with using an NDA in the game industry is that publishers typically won't sign one for you. When you begin the pitching process and working with distribution channels early on, you simply have to assume that they will keep your idea a secret. As mentioned previously, you are already protected by copyright (when your game is finished), so the chances of them stealing your idea and producing a similar product are slim-to-none.

Also, once you have secured a publisher for your game, they may flip the script and want you to sign an NDA as well! This is common practice and should not cause any concern. Much like you, they are concerned with keeping competition low and don't want rival publishers to be aware of future products.

In addition to NDAs, work out a good standard consultant agreement with an attorney—but this doesn't mean that the attorney is a consultant! It takes an attorney to actually draft a legally binding agreement for you to use. As you will have people working for you as a contractor or consultant (probably most of your employees), you need some sort of contract that basically states that all the work that the consultant does is owned by the developer (you). This document protects your IP from possible theft. Sometimes this is also known as a "work for hire" contract with a vendor or contractor.

Making sure you have a contract in place like this for every outside source for assets ensures that everything created belongs to you.

14.4   Developer and Publisher Agreements

Contracts between you and a publisher usually center around the expectations that each of you have for the other. These expectations reflect budget, schedule, and the minutia of every logistical detail regarding the development of the game. Just as you will set a schedule for external parties to deliver assets to you on schedule, a publisher will also make similar demands upon you regarding the game. The most important part of the contract, though, will focus on the ownership of the intellectual property (the game).

In this area lies the major difference between a publisher and a distributor. A publisher will essentially purchase the game and pay you for developing the product, but in the end, the publisher owns the game. Your contract will basically oversee the transfer of the IP from you (the developer) to the publisher. As publishers already have distribution channels covered, they take care of getting your game on shelves, launching a marketing campaign, and doing all the little things that ensure a game's success.

A pure distributor, however, only puts your game in stores or online for sales. Everything else will be up to you. If you are unable to make a deal with an established publisher, you will function as your own publisher (which means getting thousands of copies of your game duplicated if you intend to sell them in stores) and you will make a deal (or deals) with a distributor to circulate your game and track sales. Distributor deals focus mainly on percentages of sales that the distributor will get, locations for selling the product, and what level of distribution will take place.

Another of the many legal issues that you will face as a producer is the various contractors that work for you. Anyone that is not working directly for the company—everyone, if you are using the all-contractor business model—is a contractor. Contract artists, programmers, and so on will get your first game produced. Every single contractor requires that a contract be negotiated and drawn up. Usually, these agreements are based on "milestones" that must be met by certain dates in order for the contractor to get paid.

An example of this contract could be for an animator who is developing ten different character models for the game. There would be a different character due every ten days—basically, making a schedule of ten milestones. Every time a character model gets turned in, that animator gets a milestone payment. Sometimes, the assets being developed are called "deliverables". Either way, pay is based on performance, and all of this will be tracked as efficiently as possible through your established pipeline.

14.5   Covering the Bases

Sadly, the world of business law is a tangled jungle! We have not even scratched the surface of problems that can arise from illegal usage of licensing, end user license agreements, or the intricacies of negotiating contracts. Another legal form that you will definitely become familiar with is the "release". Every actor you use must sign a release for you to use his or her image or voice in your product— this also goes for any locations that are real places (and private property). This is why a good game attorney is a must—if not in the early stages of setting up your company and getting your concept together, then for sure when you are in the hiring and negotiating phase of getting your game made.

Finishing an awesome, cinematic game like the newest *Resident Evil* title requires a lot of planning, work, and creativity. Reproduced by permission of Capcom U.S.A., Inc. All rights reserved.

One of the most essential tasks of the producer is to become accustomed to negotiating. As mentioned in earlier chapters, developing your "soft skills" when dealing with people is just as important as keeping up on technological trends and current business practices. Negotiating the best possible deal on every single logistical aspect of your game will lower your bottom line and help guarantee the game's completion.

Good luck!

Interview: Tom Buscaglia, Game Attorney

Newman: What are some of the challenges involved with setting up a new, independent video game company/studio?

Buscaglia: Well, I always emphasize that it is more important to build a great studio than it is to build a great game. If you accomplish the former, the latter will follow. So, the most important thing, in terms of both legal and business matters, for anybody starting a new studio is for them to understand that their goal is to develop a solid, enduring business model and a business that will allow them to make their great game. And that means establishing a commitment to be serious about the success of their studio. Developers love the games they make, and I'm with them 100 percent on that, but they really need to learn to love the business part of it—at least enough to get the job done. And if they don't, then they need to find somebody else that does and work with them.

The startup developer should initially form some sort of business entity (and company or LLC [limited-liability company], for example) with the understanding that you can't sell what you don't own. So you need to set up something that's going to own the game. The second element of the model is that you have to make sure that anybody who contributes any assets to the project you're working on has legally conveyed all legal rights to those assets to the owning entity—whether it's an LLC or company/partnership. It also wouldn't be a bad idea to get an accountant, too, just to make sure that as you're doing this you're making your obligations to the government. You don't want to get off the ground and realize that you now owe the government back taxes. You'll just want to make sure you are in compliance with all employment regulations.

Newman: Are there any factors that apply specifically to setting up a video game company that independent producers would not find in generic business books?

Buscaglia: Two things. First, for the most part, the game industry is royalty-based. Second, it is all about intellectual capital. The record industry is the closest analogy to the first issue, where the record company would advance a band the money needed to record and then recoup the money from royalties. Because of this, there should be some skill involved with approaching the negotiation stages of development. Of course, not all deals as royalty-based. There's something very simple and wonderful about a work for hire deal where somebody pays you "x" amount of dollars to perform "y" amount of work, and when you're done, you're done. The royalty model is still the dominant one, because it requires a spreading of the risk and a lower initial investment. Many developers shy away from the straight "work for hire" deals, because they want to have all the upside potential income if they make a hit. The simple truth, though, is that the upside potential does not yield anything in 90 percent of the cases—or maybe more. I think way too many developers cut themselves to the bone to get a deal that's not worth taking.

As far as intellectual capital goes, don't confuse the goose with the golden egg. A top team of artists, programmers, and designers will lay lots of them. Too often, the unenlightened think that a great game franchise is where the value is, not in the team that created it. But it is all too common for a publisher to acquire a great franchise and then turn it over to an internal team that just does not have the passion or talent to pull it off. Whet they don't get is that it was the team that made the initial franchise that was great, not the game!

Newman: What's the best way then to set up your initial company? Is it filing a DBA and then incorporating later, or should you just set up an LLC from the get go?
Buscaglia: Although I am usually a great believer in the K.I.S.S. rule (Keep It Simple, Stupid!), it may not be the best way to go here. A DBA is easier, and frankly simpler, but the administrative costs of setting up a DBA or setting up an S-Corp or an LLC are not substantially different, and you're going to be better off with a formal corporate entity in the long run. If nothing else, if you succeed, you will have much better control over self-employment taxes and social security—at least in the United States—which can have a huge impact. You can put yourself on a reasonable salary and take any other profits earned as distribution of profits and not have to pay social security taxes on the income. Another reason is that if you are switching from an S-Corp to a C-Corp, you won't have to redo all the assignments of property. It's nothing to setting up your company properly—you can go to a number of Web sites, such as MyCorporation.com, that will set up your company for you for around $300. If you can't afford that, then you should probably not be trying to set up a company—you should be trying to find a job.

Newman: You offer a similar package on your Web site (http://www.gamedevkit.com), right?

Buscaglia: The GameDevKit that I developed years ago was in response to what I saw as an incredible need after attending the Indie Games Conference. I had been doing custom contributor agreements for clients over the years. But after meeting with a number of startup independent developers, I realized that these guys couldn't afford that, so I put together a package. There are articles in it about how to form a company, how to secure intellectual property—and the heart of it is a generic version of the Contributor Agreement and it is, in itself, worth way more than the $295—and there is a discount rate for ten hours of legal time, if they want to use it, which is even more valuable than the cost.

It is important that people understand the contributor agreement, though. It's the legal vehicle for transfer of ownership of assets created for the game to the company or legal entity that's going to own the game. Typically with a new game, a couple guys get together and say "Hey, lets make a game," then they get somebody to do some coding, somebody to do some artwork, and then somebody gets some music that they downloaded from the Internet—they put it all together and they think the first contract they're going to look at is a publisher deal. That doesn't work. Let's say one of the guys who did some of the original character work graduates and moves away and then you have a publisher interested in your game and they ask, "Do you own your IP?" You're pretty much dead, because you can't use the guy's artwork and you can't find him to get his written consent. You have to have some kind of written document that transfers that property to you—you can't do it by handshake agreement or anything else. It has to be assigned in writing. I kept seeing that scenario coming up with really talented people, so that was what drove me to put together my package, as well as write the articles that are available on my Web site.

Newman: How early in development should you be concerned with protecting your game with the use of trademarks and copyrights?

Buscaglia: Well, copyrights are automatic; when you create an original work, you have a copyright on it. It's not enforceable until you register it, but the ownership or the creator or author in his or her works is automatic. Trademarks don't come into play until you put something in the marketplace. You can reserve a trademark early on, but it's a more expensive process. Trademark protects your names and logos—or a specific character that's important to the game. Usually this is done after the developer secures the funding for the game—or better yet, as you may well end up conveying the game to a publisher to secure your funding, let them deal with that stuff. Chances are good that they're going to change the name of the game anyway.

Newman: When you're putting a new game together, the issue of NDAs comes up a lot. How important is it to use these?

Buscaglia: Well, for an independent developer, there are really two reasons to use them. The first is to protect you from people stealing your ideas. The other reason is to qualify the highly confidential material you are speaking about as a trade secret. You see, it is only protectable as a trade secret so long as you treat it as a trade secret. Once you tell an interested third party a trade secret, it's not a trade secret any more. Then anyone with access to these materials can use them. So, just can tell anyone who doesn't want to sign an NDA that it's not about them. It's about protecting your trade secret assets from any unscrupulous employees and contractors—and being able to enforce trade secret laws.

But, make sure that the NDA is just that; I recently had a client presented with an NDA that had a clause concerning use of his materials that included the words "including exact copy", which made me think, "If you can use the exact copy of what we are showing you without our having any recourse, where's our protection?" There wasn't any. So, at my suggestion my client blew them off. Right now, so many people are hungry for a deal that there's a tradition of people getting screwed in the game industry. I'm doing my best to make sure that this is a historical anecdote in our industry instead of the way we do business.

Newman: Once you are working with a publisher as an independent developer, what are some of the key bullet points to look for in a developer or publisher agreement?

Buscaglia: Well, this is a tough question, because it's so broad. There are hundreds of points to consider in every deal (remember, that is how I make my living!). No startup developer is going to get a triple-A contract. It won't happen. Nobody is going to give a new developer a $10 million deal to make a great game unless it's a studio composed of industry veterans who have been producing triple-A games elsewhere else for ten or fifteen years. The economic risk is too high.

Newman: What should a first-time game producer expect then from a deal?

Buscaglia: You should expect to get a deal that you can't take because it's so bad. When publishers fund a project, generally they rate their value of their funding of a project at 35–36 percent of the total net revenue from sales and licensing of the game. In reality, the value of the funding is worth more like 22–24 percent of the net revenue. In effect, the publisher is charging 50 percent more than the money's worth to lend you the money!

There are some other core issues to watch for: Does the deal involve the transfer of all intellectual property rights in the game? Do you get a percentage of ancillary revenue related to the game, like sublicenses, hint books, and even movie deals? Do you retain the rights to your tools and technology or not? I have seen some contracts where not only did the publisher take all rights to the game and any sequels, they also obtained ownership of all tools and technologies used by the developer, or developed by the developer, in the process of building the game. As a result, the developer builds no long-term value in their studio. They don't even retain the processes and procedures they used to develop the game to build their next title. Basically, you are an underpaid employee with no benefits.

Newman: So, at the very least, if you've created your own proprietary game engine for your game, you should at least try to protect that.

Buscaglia: Yes, then you retain the rights to that and the rights to exploit that you can begin to build long-term value in your studio. And if you are able to license your technology, you get the additional royalties and license fees associated with its use by third-party studios. In addition, there are a lot of other delicate points to watch for—especially with second-tier publishers or quasi-publishers that don't really do anything but provide some funding and have contacts around the world. With these guys, you sign a deal with them, then they advance you money on the game and they get worldwide rights. They don't distribute anywhere—they sublicense the game to other publishers, like a European publisher—then they get an advance and 30 percent of the royalties. Because your deal is probably 20 percent of sales with them, you are essentially getting 20 percent of their 30 percent, which is only about 6 percent of wholesale! These distributors offer nothing in the realm of marketing, but they benefit from simply having business connections. The developer should also always look for ancillary income—what I call the "lunch box bonus".

Newman: You mean merchandising?

Buscaglia: Merchandising. Movie deals. You can usually get additional potential revenue through those avenues, if you have the sense to ask for it. I usually push for a 50/50 deal in those areas.

Newman: So, is it more advantageous for a first-time producer to look at alternative means of distribution—like digital distribution or online distribution through their own site rather than a publisher? Is it better for a person to use alternative channels for their first game?

Buscaglia: Absolutely, 100 percent, yes. Direct digital distribution of your game can yield as high as a 60–70 percent royalty to the developer. And that is based on retail price, not on a net wholesale less the cost of goods (COGS). This is in contrast to a traditional publisher deal, which is probably going to be 20 percent. And if your publisher does the same thing (goes to a digital distribution channel with your game), they are going to get the 60–70 percent, and you'll just get the 20 percent of that. Do the math; that's 12 percent instead of 60 percent. Quite a bite for just setting up the deal with the online distributor!

I recommend that people get the digital distribution first. You may still need what is referred to as brick-and-mortar or retail distribution for other reasons (people still want a product in boxes). But, it's nice to have the digital distribution first, because you can then tell the brick-and-mortar publisher that you can't give them the legal rights to the IP because you already have a contract with somebody else that ties it up. But in order to do that, you will have to be able to independently fund your game without a publisher.

In this regard, the independent film industry model can be really helpful, because if we can separate the funding from the publishing, like Hollywood has with independent production companies, it would have a positive effect on the quality that we see in games and greatly benefit developers. The only problem is, you can get a bond for a movie, but try and do it for a game. As far as I know these sorts of bonded deal structures are just starting to become available.

Moreover, the revenue models for the game industry don't look that good—10 percent of the games make 90 percent of the money. Then 20 percent of the games make 95 percent of the money! That means 80 percent of the games don't make money, which means the chances of a game recuperating development costs are less than 50/50—and even if they succeed, the chances of getting any kind of return of investment that angel or venture capital investors are looking for is almost nonexistent.

Newman: At what stage should a studio look at getting legal counsel?

Buscaglia: As soon as they can afford it. I've seen too many situations where it would have been cheaper to hire me early on and to do things right, than for them to hire me later and have to pay more to me to clean everything up. It's a real, "pay me now or pay me more later" sort of industry. Part of it is the fact that startup developers just may not have the money to pay counsel when they need them, so they want to wait until later. But even if they have to do it that way, there's a ton of information available on the internet. I've done articles for Gamasutra that are also on my blog (http://www.tombuscaglia.com) concerning legal issues in the game industry. Also, the IGDA has a lot of materials in the business and legal forum, where we answer legal questions for developers.

Finally, when you are getting juniored in your first negotiation and somebody says, "That's just the way it's done in the industry", don't believe them! Every deal is a new deal and every deal is a fresh deal. It may be the way they do things, but if they cannot provide a rational basis for any deal point in a contract, then it should not be in there. And, "That's just the way thing are done, [rookie]" is *not* a good enough reason...ever.

POSTMORTEM

Rather than being any kind of all-inclusive manual for creating cinematic games, I hope that this book will serve as a jumping-off point for you. With game developers and publishers out there already starting to tap into the vast sea of filmmaking techniques for their games (just check out all the screenshots in this book), the promise of future cinematic games is at an all-time high. I hope that young producers and creative directors (as well as game designers) will utilize all the awesome filmmaking books and Web sites out there that focus on great storytelling, cinematography, character development, and directing (there are many available on the Focal Press Web site, http://www.focalpress.com). Just remember that when you make a cinematic game, you do not have to take anything away from game play. When using this book, or any other filmmaking or game design book, great features, a fun interface, and awesome game play are a must for any truly successful game. The strategies and techniques featured in this book should assist you in your quest to make your game more immersive and more rewarding and to broaden your game's potential for crossover development.

In closing, I would like to say that the creation of this book would not have been possible without all the help I received from Focal Press (specifically Laura Lewin, Georgia Kennedy, and Chris Simpson), the interviewees contained within these pages (special thanks to Ray Pena), and the contributions I received from the game developers and publishers who supplied me with the wonderful screenshots herein, which are so indicative of the type of development I discuss. I would also like to thank Lee Ann Newman, Scott Biggs, and Elsevier Publishing. Your support was instrumental in the completion of this book. Thank you all!

APPENDIX

APPENDIX A: EXTRAS

A lot of various reports, forms, and spreadsheets are used during the production of a video game. This appendix provides a collection of some of the more important paperwork, as well as the forms that are most often associated with the film industry—forms you will use during production of your cinematic game. Keep in mind, though, that any legal forms should be looked over by a local attorney before you use them on a project.

Sample Game Design/Concept

Your basic design document/concept is like a presentation. It should include a few strategic photos and the like to support the written materials. Make sure to include all key details within the game that will make it sell and unique.

Game Title

Be creative when coming up with your game title. It is one of your first marketing tools and should define the type of game you are creating, as well as generate excitement.

Table of Contents

Here you will list the sections of your game concept/design. Fine tune the major points within the sections with a numerical system like the table of contents for this book: 1.1, 1.2, 1.3, etc.

1. Overview

This section should lay out what the game is basically about. Include details regarding the story, the protagonist (and other key characters), key features, and the genre the game will be marketed under. Also be sure to note anything that will differentiate your game from the field and what platforms the game will be developed for.

2. Gameplay

Here you will breakdown how the game actually works; is it a race against time or against opponents? What different abilities, levels, etc. are involved in the game? What's the scoring system? How many different skill levels will there be? Will there be online play? Lay out the who, what, where, when, and how of the game as well.

3. Interface and Control

This is the section where you lay out the main menus and what the controller will do. Also, any features contained within the game that are outside of the actual gameplay, such as maps, weapon selection screens, and so on should be laid out in this section. If you are utilizing a type of controller other than the standardD-pad type for most consoles (or keyboard for PC), be sure to mention this as well.

4. Graphics

Here you will describe the various artistic elements of the game. Will it be photorealistic or cartoon-style? What different models, environments, and props will be featured in the game? Also lay out the lighting and camera style of the game.

6. Artificial Intelligence

How will the enemies react in the game? Are they passive or aggressive? What about game-controlled teammates? What will be the intelligence levels of all NPC's within the environment?

7. Environment

Talk about the various locales/levels of the game, and any environmental elements that will affect gameplay. Does the game terrain vary? What about weather? How does it affect the characters or missions?

8. Editors

How much customization is involved with the game? How is it done? If you are planning add-on packs or maps, mention these here.

While this is not an all-inclusive design document, it will cover most game types or genres. If you are going to make an arcade/casual game, you won't need most of these sections—modify the document to fit the needs of your game. You can also add other optional items such as information regarding the actual game studio (like your mission statement).

Production Flowchart

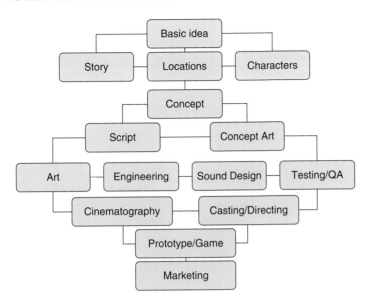

Sample Basic Schedule

Name of Project		
Platforms:	Xbox360	PS3
Release:	Spring	2009

Phase of Development (Weeks)	Low Estimate	High Estimate	Avg Estimate	Probable
Planning and Brainstorming	4	10	7	8
Pre-Production and Script	4	10	7	8
Design	16	22	18	20
Art	22	30	26	27
Engineering	30	40	35	36
Sound	6	8	7	7
QA	10	12	11	11
Post Production	10	20	15	16
Project Totals				

Sample Budget

Name of Project			
Expense	**Amount**	**Cost**	**Total**
Personnel per Dept			
Engine			
Software Licenses			
Hardware			
Studio Expenses			
Misc.			

This spreadsheet would breakdown all the personnel per department—including art, programming/engineering, QA, sound, and so on—and breakdown their pay per position for the project. You would also list all software, including engine, and include those costs as well. Finally, you would breakdown all the hardware that must be purchased, any rentals that must be done (to include external studios for sound or mocap), and all the expenses associated with running the studio.

Once you have included all this information, per department this spreadsheet will be about four-five pages long!

Sample Staffing Plan

This section will basically list every position you need filled for development. Simply plug in the title, responsibility, any specific skills that must be fulfilled by this person, and the duration of employment.

Role	Project Responsibility	Skills Required	Number Required	Start Date	Hire Duration

This section is where you put the actual people hired to fill each position (later becomes an org chart), date of hire, expected termination of contract, their rate of pay, unit of pay, and where they were hired from.

Role	Name	Requested FTE FY05-06	Acquired FTE FY05-06	Rate	Rate Unit	Source
Total						

Sample Script Breakdown

Scene #	Scene name	Breakdown page #
Description		Int. or Ext.
Script page		Day or night

CAST	EXTRAS	EXTRAS/ATMOSPHERE

PROPS	WARDROBE	MAKE-UP/HAIR

VEHICLES	SPECIAL EQUIPMENT	SOUND FX/MUSIC

Sample Character Breakdown

A character breakdown basically lists all the information regarding a specific character within your game. It will be used by the actors you will cast to understand the motivation and style of the character, as well as make sure the director keeps the actors on point. It is also useful for screenwriters as a reference when making decisions in the story regarding that character. You would make a character breakdown for all major characters in the game with as much detail as is deemed necessary. Here are the typical areas you would fill in for each character:

1. Character Function. Is he/she the protagonist, antagonist, or a supporting role?
2. Character's Major Emotions. What is the general mood of the character?
3. Character's Background. This can include birthplace, context of appearance in the script, and general motivation.
4. Character's Objectives. Does the character live or die? What's the goal?
5. Script Notes. List the places in the script that the character appears and the significance of these scenes.
6. Character's Dialogue. If possible, list the dialogue for that character; if it is a major character, you would attach the entire script.

Remember that your writer will have the major role in determining the information listed above and that you should heed their suggestions. Character breakdowns, when coupled with the script, are a great tool for getting top notch performances out of your actors and screenwriters.

INTERVIEW CREDITS

1-1 Interview: Noah Falstein

"Reproduced by permission of Noah Falstein."

1-2 Interview: Warren Spector

"Reproduced by permission of Warren Spector."

1-3 Interview: Ray Pena

"Reproduced by permission of Ray Pena."

1-4 Interview: Ron Burke

"Reproduced by permission of Ronald Gene Burke."

2-5 Interview: Daniel Erickson

"Reproduced by permission of Daniel Erickson."

2-6 Interview: Mathieu Raynault

"Reproduced by permission of Mathieu Raynault."

2-7 Interview: Bruce Block

"Reproduced by permission of Bruce Block."

2-8 Interview: Bob Sabiston

"Reproduced by permission of Bob Sabiston."

2-9 Interview: Donise Hardy

"Reproduced by permission of Donise L. Hardy."

2-10 Interview: Jay Duplass

"Reproduced by permission of Jay Duplass."

2-11 Interview: Marc Schaefgen

"Reproduced by permission of Marc Schaefgen."

3-12 Interview: Richard Rouse III

"Reproduced by permission of Richard Rouse III."

3-13 Interview: Patrick Hamilton

"Reproduced by permission of Patrick Hamilton."

3-14 Interview: Tom Buscaglia

"Reproduced by permission of Thomas H. Buscaglia."

BIBLIOGRAPHY

It's always difficult to remember exactly where some things were learned—especially when you have worked in both the film and game industries for so long. Over the years, I have attended numerous conferences, read countless books, pored over even more Web sites, and interviewed dozens of my peers—and this is in addition to my general education! Though most game concepts are universally used and accepted throughout the industry, some sources have done a better job than others at communicating these ideas.

Here is a list of books that, in my opinion, can expand upon the knowledge contained within these pages and assist you in your endeavors. This list also contains the books that are specifically mentioned within this text.

Ahearn, Luke. *3D Game Textures: Create Professional Game Art Using Photoshop*, Focal Press, Boston, Massachusetts, 2006.

Block, Bruce. *The Visual Story: Seeing the Structure of Film, TV, and New Media*, Focal Press, Boston, Massachusetts, 2007.

Chandler, Heather. *The Game Production Handbook*, Charles River Media, Hingham, Massachusetts, 2006.

Clurman, Harold. *On Directing*, Fireside Books, New York, 1972.

Field, Syd. *Screenplay: The Foundations of Screenwriting*, Delta/Dell Publishing, New york, 2005.

Figgis, Mike. *Digital Filmmaking*, Faber and Faber, New York, 2007.

Hawkins, Brian. *Real-Time Cinematography for Games*, Charles River Media, Hingham, Massachusetts, 2005.

Irish, Dan. *The Game Producer's Handbook*, Premier Press/Thomson Course Technology PTR, Boston, 2005.

Isbister, Katherine. *Better Game Characters by Design*, Morgan Kaufmann Publishers, Inc, San Francisco, 2006.

Katz, Steven D. *Film Directing Shot by Shot*, Michael Wiese Productions, Studio City, California, 1991.

Laramee, Francois Dominic. *Game Design Perspectives*, Charles River Media, Hingham, Massachusetts, 2002.

Marx, Christy. *Writing for Animation, Comics, and Games*, Focal Press, Boston, Massachusetts, 2007.

Mascelli, Joseph V. *The Five C's of Cinematography: Motion Picture Filming Techniques*, Silman-James Press, Los Angeles, California, 1998.

McKee, Robert. *Story: Substance, Structure, Style and The Principles of Screenwriting*, Regan Books, New York, 1997.

Neumann, John von, and Morgenstern, Oskar. *Theory of Games and Economic Behavior*, Princeton University Press, Princeton, New Jersey, 2007.

Pressman, Roger S. *Software Engineering: A Practitioner's Approach*, McGraw-Hill Science, 2004.

Schwaber, Ken, and Beedle, Mike. *Agile Software Development with SCRUM*, Prentice Hall, 2001.

GLOSSARY

AFTRA Abbreviation for the American Federation of Television and Radio Artists. A union that represents people who work in the entertainment industry.

Alpha Test The process of evaluating the initial version of a game.

Antagonist A character in a story that is in direct conflict with the main character, the protagonist.

Artificial Intelligence Software that is designed to create realistic motion and actions by non-player characters or entities within a game.

ASC Abbreviation for the American Society of Cinematographers. An organization for directors of photography and camera operators.

Aspect Ratio The ratio of the width to the height of a screen image.

Asset Any individual element used in game development, such as a piece of art, a character, a sample, etc.

Beta Test The process of testing the final version of a game before it is released to the publisher. Sometimes can be open to the public and is primarily for working out final bugs and issues.

Blocking Setting up the motion and movement of elements within a scene.

Bug A flaw in a game's coding that creates an error in game play.

Build Another name for a particular version of a game. A game is usually called a new build when significant new assets are added.

Casting The process of auditioning actors for particular roles.

CERO Abbreviation for the Computer Entertainment Rating Organization. The game rating system for Japan.

CGI Abbreviation for Computer Generated Imagery. Denotes any image or character made artificially using programming, coding, or software.

Character Breakdown A sheet that tells the basic background information of a character. Used for casting purposes.

Cinematic Often used in the game industry as another name for a cut-scene. When used as an adjective, it denotes using techniques or style indicative of a movie.

Cinematography The art of using light and color for artistic value in front of a camera, or in a piece of media.

Close-up A camera shot that fills the frame with the subject. In the case of a person, the subject's head or head/shoulders.

Closing Kit A series of files that include all the information used to create a game. Usually stored for future use on additional localizations or re-release of the game.

Code Release Another name for the Gold Master phase of game development.

CODEC Abbreviation for Compressor/Decompressor. Usually a plug-in program or algorithm that handles audio and/or video.

Coding The process of actually programming the code used to make a game.

Composition The artistic design of individual elements with a camera shot. In a game, it is the same process within the frame of a game level.

Continuity The process of keeping track of the logistics of a shot in order to make sure scenes are consistent and will cut together.

Copyright The legal protection of a particular piece of intellectual property.

Coverage Getting enough material of a particular scene or location to ensure a great end result.

Cutaway A camera shot of something that is not involved with the main action in the scene—usually moving the camera to a key prop or location that will be used later.

Cut-scene A game industry term for a piece of action within the game that is watched rather than played by the gamer.

Deliverable Any individual piece of work that must be submitted by a third party to a developer—to include art, code, etc.

Depth of Field The amount of the frame that will be in focus.

Developer The party that is actually developing and producing a game.

Director of Photography The person who is in charge of lighting, the cameras, and in some cases, the artistic look of a project.

Engine The main program or software that determines and works with the motion graphics of a game.

ESRB Abbreviation for the Entertainment Software Rating Board. The current rating system in the United States for video games.

EULA Abbreviation for End User License Agreement. The contract between a game publisher and a game retailer.

Exposure The amount of light that is allowed to hit the film in a camera. In the game world, it means altering the look of a scene accordingly.

Frame To compose the area of a scene that will be on camera. Also called framing or framing a shot.

Gold Master The final version of a game that is turned in to the publisher.

IGDA Abbreviation for the International Game Developers Association. A group for individuals who work in game development to interact.

Intellectual Property A legally protected idea or work that has been created, to include key characters and property.

Lens The glass or series of pieces of glass that are in front of the camera. In the game world, it means choosing the style of focus and framing to create a virtual lens style.

Localization Adapting a game to a particular language or locale.

Master Shot A camera shot that is taken far away from the subject in order to get the entire location in view.

Middleware Software developed by third parties in order to add functionality within game development.

Milestone Usually a significant achievement during the development of a game that represents meeting a deadline in the game's schedule.

Mod Short for either 'modification' or 'module.' Mods are small bits of programming done by third parties to enhance already present games.

Montage A series of different shots that represent a single piece of action or juxtaposes simultaneous, separate events.

Motion Capture The process of attaching an actor to electronic equipment designed to record movement for use within a game.

Non-disclosure Agreement A contract, usually between an employer and employee, that is meant to discourage divulging any details of a particular game in development.

Pan Moving the camera horizontally to follow action. The same action can be duplicated in a game using the same motion.

PEGI Abbreviation for Pan European Game Information board. The rating system for games in most of Europe.

Pipeline The path that has been designated for individual assets to take in order to facilitate the game's development.

Pitch A short dialogue created to sell an idea or game to a developer or publisher.

Platform The hardware systems that the game will be created for.

Postmortem A meeting that is usually held at the end of development to evaluate what was done correctly and incorrectly during production. Used to help future projects.

Prop Means 'property.' Any physical item used within a scene, to include the actual scenery.

Protagonist The main character in a story.

Prototype Usually a playable, short version of a game used to sell it to a publisher. Can also function as a demo for the public.

Publisher The entity that is responsible for duplicating the game for sales to the public an retailers, as well as marketing and promoting that game.

R&D Abbreviation for Research and Development. This is a phase during game development where the concept is honed, or can also indicate a department that is responsible for new technologies.

Rule of Thirds The practice of framing a shot where key elements lie along the intersection of three horizontal and three diagonal lines that equally divide the frame.

Quality Assurance The department that is responsible for tracking and assessing all bugs and areas of game play.

SAG Abbreviation for Screen Actors Guild. This is a union that represents stage and screen actors.

Sampling The process of recording small bits of sound for use within a game.

Scene An individual portion of a script that usually centers around one piece of action or one location.

Script The actual written story, including dialogue, that is used for a piece of work in the entertainment industry.

Scrum The use of small meetings within game development to keep the team informed and working in sync.

Shot List A list of individual camera shots that will be included in a scene. Usually made by the director, though the

cinematographer also gets involved in the film world.

Shutter Speed The speed at which the camera's shutter rotates. In the game world, it means altering the image to imitate the look of the process in a movie.

Sides A small piece of a script (usually one or two pages) used for casting purposes.

Staging Setting up the individual elements within a scene.

Storyboard A drawing or piece of art used to illustrate how a scene will be shot.

Structure The format of a script or story that best tells the action within a medium.

Symbolism The use of props or locations within a story to represent a greater idea or theme.

Theme The underlying idea that the story represents.

Three Point Lighting The standard in lighting when working with video or film. Usually means a light will be positioned in front of, in back of, and to the side of the subject.

Tilt To move the camera vertically to follow the action. The same action can be duplicated within a game.

Trademark A legally protected piece of intellectual property that usually is a symbol or logo.

USK Abbreviation for Unterhaltungssoftware Selbstkontrolle. This is the rating board for games in Germany.

User Interface Any part of the game that allows the gamer to input or receive information or data. Examples include the menu and in-game status information.

Voiceover The process of recording actors' voices for use within a game.

WGA Abbreviation for Writers Guild of America. A union that represents writers in the entertainment industry.

INDEX